Intersectionality in the Muslim South Asian-American Middle Class

Intersectionality in the Muslim South Asian-American Middle Class

Lifestyle Consumption beyond Halal and Hijab

Farha Bano Ternikar

LEXINGTON BOOKS
Lanham • Boulder • New York • London

Published by Lexington Books

An imprint of The Rowman & Littlefield Publishing Group, Inc.
4501 Forbes Boulevard, Suite 200, Lanham, Maryland 20706
www.rowman.com

6 Tinworth Street, London SE11 5AL, United Kingdom

Copyright © 2021 The Rowman & Littlefield Publishing Group, Inc.

All rights reserved. No part of this book may be reproduced in any form or by any electronic or mechanical means, including information storage and retrieval systems, without written permission from the publisher, except by a reviewer who may quote passages in a review.

British Library Cataloguing in Publication Information Available

Library of Congress Cataloging-in-Publication Data

Names: Ternikar,Farha, 1970- author. Title: Intersectionality in the Muslim South Asian American middle class : lifestyle consumption beyond halal and hijab / Farha Bano Ternikar. Description : Lexington Books, [2021] | Includes bibliographical references and index. | Summary: "This book examines the use of everyday items such as good, clothing, and social media accounts to offer sociological and intersectional analyses of how religion, race, politics, class, and gender shape, define, and reinforce consumption practices of Muslim American women" —Provided by publisher. Identifiers: LCCN 2021043250 (print) | LCCN 2021043251 (ebook) | ISBN 9781793649393 (cloth) | | ISBN 9781793649416 (paperback) ISBN 9781793649409 (epub) Subjects: LCSH: Muslim women—United States—Ethnic identity. | South Asian American women—Ethnic identity. | Middle class Muslims—United States—Ethnic identity. | Muslim women—United States—Social conditions. | South Asian American women—Social conditions. | Middle class Muslims—United States—Social conditions. Classification: LCC HQ1170 .T46 2021 (print) | LCC HQ1170 (ebook) | DDC 305.48/6970973—dc23 LC record available at https://lccn.loc.gov.2021043250 LC ebook record available at https://lccn.loc.gov/2021043251

Contents

Preface	vii
Acknowledgments	ix
Introduction	1
Chapter 1: Beyond Authentic Curry and Halal Kebobs	17
Chapter 2: Bicultural Identities, Prada Bags, and Saris?	43
Chapter 3: Haute Hijab, Brown Girl, and the Consumption of Social Media	67
Conclusion	97
References	109
Index	119
About the Author	125

Preface

I did not get married in a sari.

I was married in Chicago at my sister's house in Naperville. I was a graduate student at the time, and even though I was raised in a middle-class Indian Muslim household in the United States, I didn't want a big fat wedding.

But I did want a perfect wedding cake, and I wanted to be married wearing a lengha.

In 2002, my perfect wedding cake was a small cake that was tasteful and not from a grocery store but from a bakery in the city, and it was definitely not plain vanilla.

My lengha was just ready made bought from Devon Avenue,[1] also known as Little India in Chicago.

Though I knew I didn't want a sari, I actually wasn't so particular about the lengha—just not red or white.

Lenghas or saris are traditionally worn over salwar kameezes by North Indian brides. It was also my family's tradition to wear lenghas over saris since we are Indian Muslims and lenghas are more modest than saris.

Like many women in the Indian and Pakistani Muslim American communities, I have always placed a high value on food and shopping.

When I was a child, my mother taught me how to shop; she also taught me, what was halal or zabiha, and what was Indian or Pakistani. She also tried to teach me how to cook.

When I talk with Pakistani and Indian Muslim American female friends, we talk about the latest hate crime against a Muslim community in New Zealand and the fear we have for our mothers or sisters wearing hijab. We dissect the latest trends in modest, Desi or Western attire.

We share conversations about making healthy food for our families if it happens to be halal, organic or local, and discuss the lifestyle blogs that highlight Desi food or multicultural fashion.

And when my sisters ask what this book is about, I saw in a lot of ways it's about us but in a lot of ways it's about all women.

As Desi women, what we eat, buy or wear often challenges Orientalist stereotypes. It may reinforce gendered norms or resist cultural assimilation, but what we consume definitely says something about who we are or who we wish we were.

By the same token, consumption creates community. Whether we shop with friends face to face in brick-and-mortar stores, or converse and buy online, or share links from Instagram, the consumption patterns of South Asian Muslim American women are always part of a broader community. I hope that I have introduced both these consumers and their communities in this book.

NOTE

1. Devon Avenue is a neighborhood on the Northside of Chicago, which is home to South Asian restaurants, shops and salons. Chapter 1 provides a brief history.

Acknowledgments

Like all feminist and intersectional academics, I could not have written this without the support of many people.

First, I am grateful to all the South Asian Muslim American women who shared their stories and time with me. Without them, this project would not have possible.

I also want to thank those who read early drafts of chapters including Carol Fadda-Conrey, Asmaa Malik, Dana Olwan, Alice Julier, Rachel Schwartz and Megan Elias. I am grateful for their friendships and feedback.

I am grateful to the many scholars and friends that inspired me to finish this project including my mentor, Tamara Sonn, Psyche Forson, Junko Takedo, Saher Selod, Kathleen Costello-Sullivan, Julie Olin-Ammentorp and Jennifer Glancy. I also thank both Jesse Nissim and Lauren Senesac Nichols for their careful editing and proofreading at different stages of the manuscript.

I must thank the Sociology Department at Loyola University Chicago where I learned to conduct field work through the mentorship of Judith Wittner and Fred Kniss. I am grateful to Le Moyne College including Gender and Women's Studies, Research and Development grants, and the campus librarians.

I also benefited from the Feast and Famine seminar at New York University which helped plant the seeds of this project many years ago; the Food Studies Department at Syracuse University where I presented early chapters of this book; and the Eastern Sociological Society where I first discussed this project with Sharon Zukin.

I must acknowledge *Feminist Food Studies: Intersectional Perspectives* edited by Barbara Parker, Jennifer Brady, Elaine Power, Susan Belyea which features an earlier draft of chapter 1 on food and consumption.

I am also thankful to my mother for teaching me to value my bicultural identity through my salwar kameezes as much as through her biryani recipes, to my sisters for encouraging me to finish during a very difficult two years, and to my nieces, Junnah and Lailah.

Last, but not least, I am grateful to my fellow sociologist and husband, Travis Vande Berg. Over the process of writing this book, he continued to give me critical and analytical feedback on the project, endless support and patience and many homemade curries and cookies.

Introduction
Beyond Desi Divas and Halal Housewives

Junnah Khan is traveling for work this month. She is wearing hijab and knows that when she flies, she has to budget extra time for screening. Junnah wears the turban-style hijab, which covers her hair but leaves her neck and ears exposed. She's wearing her slip-on Converse sneakers but packed her Tory Burch pumps for her first meeting. As she's waiting to go through the electronic screener, she puts her carry-on, laptop, cell phone, Louis Vuitton purse, and Gucci sunglasses in the blue bins. Her bracelet, which she didn't remove, sets off the scanner. It's a priceless Indian gold bangle from her mother.

INTRODUCTION

The vignette above illustrates how multiple modes of social status simultaneously shape the dress and wardrobes of immigrant women. Junnah, a 45-year-old Indian Muslim American woman, chooses to wear the bangle, which is symbolic of her Indian nationality, her gender, and her social class. Even in a post-9/11 society and under an administration that is hostile to immigrants from non-European nations, Junnah chooses to wear the hijab, a marker of her religious identity. However, her wardrobe choices also reflect her career, class, and culture.

"Desi girlfriends, do you have a uniform?" I asked on Facebook in 2016, and I received a slew of responses identifying particular items, including J.Crew and Tory Burch flats, Celine and Prada bags, and Gucci and Ray-Ban sunglasses. "Desi" is the insider slang word for South Asian immigrants, and middle-class Desi women's wardrobes are embedded with buzzwords of status consumption like the brands noted above (Mir 2014). But like many immigrant women, especially those who achieve upward social mobility in the second generation, SAMA (South Asian Muslim American) women must reconcile the different and sometimes contradictory kinds of status they inhabit, including those determined by gender, race, and social class, and those imposed by tradition or religion (Khan and Hermansen 2009).

South Asian culture, especially in Pakistani and North Indian Muslim traditions, plays an important role in shaping the consumption patterns of SAMA women, including the college-educated, middle-to upper-class women I have interviewed. Some of these women wear hijab even though they are aware of their racial and religious minority status in a society that is diverse but not always welcoming or even tolerant of Muslim or non-white immigrants. Others maintain modesty in hybrid ways by not wearing hijab but only wearing long skirts, pants, or loose garments. Some SAMA women interpret modesty in their restrained use of makeup or jewelry.

It was necessary to take into account the changes in the American political climate as I developed this research, but I did not want to reduce SAMA women to the hijab or other essentialist symbols as the media often do. I found that SAMA women have developed sophisticated and nuanced understandings of politics, capitalism, and collective identity, and consumption that go far beyond debates over hijab, ethnic clothing, halal food, and work-life balance. Through conversations with SAMA women in their homes and in coffee shops, restaurants, and mosques, I began to understand the agency SAMA women have in their consumption practices, the structures within which they exercise this agency, and why shopping is for them much more than a gendered activity.

The consumption and shopping practices of second-generation South Asian Muslim women are integral in negotiating their collective identities. From cooking and ordering authentic South Asian halal food in local markets to purchasing wardrobes that combine Western trends with traditional ethnic clothing, SAMA women are crafting new types of identities shaped by both conspicuous consumption and the pursuit of distinction (Veblen 1899/2006; Bourdieu 1984; Zukin and Macquire 2004; Srinivas 2006; Mir 2014). Their consumption habits are shaped by social class, ethnicity, gender, religion, and sometimes also politics. This new interdisciplinary work builds on W.E.B. Du Bois's (1903) theory of "triple consciousness," as SAMA women are religiously modest, socioeconomically middle class, and "authentically" bicultural.

Status consumption is a multidimensional phenomenon driven by both ethnicity and immigrant status in an ever-changing politically and ethnically diverse society. Transnational migrants like South Asian Muslims construct their own consumer culture by using their ethno-religious traditions, dominant commercial cultures, social media, and identity markers that they somehow piece together from the gender, religious, ethnic, and social class communities in which they live. SAMA women's consumption and cultural patterns are distinct from those of other American women. In adapting American culture to conform with Islamic modesty norms and halal food restrictions, SAMA women consume in ways that preserve ethnic wardrobes and ethnic food traditions. Adherence to practices of wearing hijab or other garments traditionally used in maintaining modesty is best understood on a continuum from conservative or orthodox to liberal (Mir 2014). Respondents in my study bring up consumption practices related to hijab and halal. Halal practices are consumption practices of food according to Islamic law, and these dietary practices are varied. Maintaining halal practices depended on geographies, technology, and historical period (Armanios and Ergene 2018).

BEYOND INTERSECTIONALITY: THEORETICAL FRAMEWORK

I use transnational feminist theory and consumption theory to frame my argument, and I am attentive to intersectionality as it shapes my research participants' experiences (Crenshaw 1989; Collins 1990; Forson-Williams and Wilkerson 2011). Turning to the foundational framework from Kimberle Crenshaw and Patricia Hills Collins (2011), intersectionality emphasizes the need to go beyond a gender analysis in order to explore how patriarchy and gender inequality work in interaction with race, class, and sexuality as interlocking modes of oppression. In 2015, Patricia Hills Collins wrote, "The term intersectionality references the critical insight that race, class, gender, sexuality, ethnicity, nation, ability, and age operate not as unitary, mutually exclusive entities, but as reciprocally constructing phenomena that in turn shape complex inequalities" (Collins and Chepp 2015, 2). Contemporary intersectionality is a theoretical paradigm that is ever-changing and often is in conversation with transnational feminism, particularly with non-Western understandings of gender and feminism (Narayan 1997). Purkayashtana (2012, 613) adds a transnational layer to intersectionality, "Understanding and attending to the complexities of transnationalism—composed of structures within, between and across nation-states, and virtual spaces—alerts us to look for other axes of domination and the limits of using 'women of color' concepts, as we use them now, to look across and within nation-states to understand the impact of transnationalism." Transnational feminism does not assume a centrality of a Euro-American, Christian, or white middle-class understanding of gender or feminist theory (Narayan 1997; Narayan and Purkayasthana 2009; Purkayastha 2012).

Psyche Forson-Williams (2011) has added that intersectionality is an important theoretical paradigm to understand women's lives and consumption. I add religion and immigrant status to this framework in my analysis of how foodways, ethnic wardrobes, and social media highlight collective identities in the American context, especially in our current political climate. I apply intersectionality to the racialized and gendered "Desi" performance that takes place within immigrant communities. While SAMA women experience evaluation by the outside, often xenophobic world, they also are evaluated by their own communities for how authentic, religious, and sometimes even how political their wardrobe and food choices are.

New research on racialization and American Muslims further demonstrates how American Muslims also develop double consciousness, especially in a post-9/11 era (Du Bois 1903; Selod and Garner 2016). Saher Selod (2018, 21) highlights that "[s]tudying the surveillance of Muslim Americans enables an understanding of how their religious identity undergoes racialization." In her analysis of American Muslims after 9/11, Selod explains that in addition to physical characteristics and skin color, the study of racialization of American Muslims by majority groups must include cultural traits such as dress style and gender if we are to understand how racialization plays out in the everyday lives of Muslim Americans (24). Racialization is the making of race where it previously was not a way people thought about themselves — and though we think of racialization as being based in physical characteristics of the body, race is also constructed around other visible cues. For example, American Muslim women who wear hijab or American Muslim men who wear beards are more likely to be harassed, even if they are white or light skinned, than those who do not display religious or cultural garb.

Building on Du Bois, Selod's work explores how American Muslims, especially since 9/11, are also made up of "multiple selves" as they shift their identities in public spaces because of surveillance; this has a resulted in a climate of anxiety and fear. Narratives of anxiety have been present since the 1990s for Indian immigrants as Tulasi Srinivas (2006) notes. Srivinas emphasizes the anxiety associated with immigration in the diaspora for Indian immigrants who try to maintain ethnic and cultural identities associated with homelands. Since 9/11, and then under the Trump administration, narratives of anxiety for Muslim Americans have been heightened because of Islamophobia and surveillance (Selod 2018).

CONSUMPTION THEORY: BEYOND VEBLEN AND BOURDIEU

The classical sociological views of consumer culture, including those of Thorstein Veblen and Pierre Bourdieu should be complicated by scholars with the arrival and integration of transnational migrants, especially those from racialized and religious populations. This project builds on Veblen's (1899/2006) theories of society and conspicuous consumption, Bourdieu's (1984) understanding of taste, and Sharon Zukin's (2004) research on shopping. Veblen shows that items of material culture, including clothes, are social markers (1899/2006) and consumption is linked to status: "Since the consumption of these more excellent goods is an evidence of wealth, it becomes honorific; and conversely, the failure to consume in due quantity and quality becomes a mark of inferiority and demerit" (1899/2006). Over a century ago, Veblen explained that middle-class Americans signal their wealth through "conspicuous consumption," a term used by sociologists to describe overt status-signaling through acquiring material goods. In terms of SAMA middle-class immigrants, clothing, accessories, and jewelry can all be analyzed as examples of conspicuous consumption Conspicuous consumption is not the only factor shaping SAMA wardrobes, however; as I demonstrate in chapter 2, they are shaped by social and cultural capital. Cultural capital influences taste, and taste influences consumption. However, the consumption habits of middle- and upper-class South Asian immigrants are also shaped by Veblen's notion of competitive and conspicuous consumption. The SAMA women in my study not only engage in competitive consumption with their professional peers by keeping up with Western designer fashions, but they also compete with the women in their ethnic, religious, and immigrant communities by shopping for salwar kameez, hijabs, and jewelry.

Bourdieu (1984) argues that through cultural capital, Americans develop taste, which further shapes their consumption patterns while signaling status. Taste is a result of cultural capital that is passed on through families, schools, communities, and other social institutions. Cultural capital, in addition to economic and social capital, shapes consumption. The social capital includes multiple social networks that SAMA women are a part of. For SAMA women in particular, social capital from South Asian and Muslim immigrant communities and extended family plays an enhanced role in gaining access to ethnic boutiques, clothing from abroad, and private home clothing sales, as well as immigrant foodways. As SAMA women accumulate their bicultural wardrobes, cultural capital and displays of conspicuous consumption are significant; accumulated items may be as various as salwar kameezes,[1] bangles, hijabs, dresses, tunics, skinny jeans, earrings, and designer shoes and bags.

The salwar kameezes, bangles, and earrings are indicative of capital related to their ethnic identities, and Western clothing, and bags are capital within the overall American middle-class landscape.

In *Point of Purchase,* Sharon Zukin (2004) puts forth the idea that shopping is central to our social lives in part because helps create and maintain relationships and social hierarchies. Zukin's research informs my work, as she highlights how shopping gains much more significance than mere economic exchange when analyzed in the context of social relationships and social status: "Shopping with a sister not only provides you with a ready-made mentor, it also creates a special form of intimacy" (54). In other words, shopping creates bonds, especially in female relationships. As Zukin states, "Shopping gives us a common frame of reference for checking each other out. Look at the way middle-class parents ask where your children go to school, or teenagers ask each other where they bought their jeans" (38). For SAMA women, learning to shop is embedded in class privilege and shaped by ethnic, gendered, and religious identities. Second-generation middle-class SAMA women grew up going shopping as a leisure activity, which included shopping for jeans at the mall but also learning to appreciate salwar kameezes at cultural shopping bazaars. Learning to shop, researching luxury accessories, shopping for status, and displaying the cultural capital to acquire hard-to-find ethnic items all resonated in my own research (Zukin 2004, 61).

Zukin and Macquire (2004) also introduced us to the world of online shopping in 2004 as it is first starting to take off with Amazon.com and eBay. Their article highlights the importance of consumer culture: "Consumer culture certainly provides a universal toolkit, a material and symbolic repertoire, for expressing collective identities. But consumer culture provides tools for resistance as well as for integration and adaptation" (2004, 189). Immigrants and racialized minorities continue to use consumption to challenge the hegemonic negative or false stereotypes about them but also to assimilate, as many anthropologists have also shown (Chin 2001; Shankar 2015).

Contemporary scholars show how consumption is linked to race and immigration. Elizabeth Chin's (2001), Arlene Davila's (2001), Anita Mannur's (2010), and Shalani Shankar's (2008) work on race, ethnicity, and collective ethnic identity shed light on how consumption is also used by racial minorities and U.S. immigrants to negotiate collective racial or immigrant identities. Chin highlights the link between race and consumption in her work on African Americans. Davila explores how Hispanic Americans also construct collective identity through consumption. Shankar's research explores Desi youth consumption in Silicon Valley.

Chin's (2001, 3) research on consumption and African American children emphasizes how race, class, and gender materialize through consumption. Chin's immersive ethnographic research on African American consumers is a significant contribution to the scholarship on culture, consumption, and community because she examines how history and geography in addition to race, gender, and class help shape consumption for African American children. Through participant observation with Black children, she demonstrates how Black girls in particular buy and play with white dolls and transform them into their own. Her research on African Americans challenges the negative stereotypes that non-Black Americans have had of Black children as brand-obsessed, pathological over-consumers. She states that "[c]hildren on the whole did not seem driven by their impulses. Kids often managed to buy an astonishing amount for twenty dollars and overall they were careful, thoughtful, and critical of their buying" (131). Chin also emphasizes that consumption is a social experience, especially for girls who use shopping as a way to maintain relationships and show concerns for others, including family members. Chin concludes that consumption is embedded in politics and social inequality, especially for black children. In chapter 3, I further examine how consumption is also a social experience for SAMA women.

Davila's research on Latinos in American society emphasizes the importance of distinct cultural identities, ethnicity, and marketing for both political and societal reasons. Marketing flattens these identities and often uses skin tone, Spanish language, and reductionist understandings of cultural identities by lumping Cubans, Mexicans, Puerto Ricans, and Dominicans in the same marketing audience, which often attempts to market products to these distinct ethnic groups. Davila also highlights the problematic politics of authenticity surrounding fluency in Spanish and "Latino" origin, which creates biases toward the foreign-born, and erases U.S.-born and English-speaking Hispanic and Latino identity (Davila 2001, 78–79).

Davila's study emphasizes the significance of "consumer culture" for producing new racial or ethnic identities but notes that the effects of consumer culture are uneven. U.S. racial hierarchies, along with politics of immigration, shape the marketing to "Latinos." Davila asserts, "These are the Hispanics we can market to but also expel or banish, who will remain in their place within their culture: the nation within the nation that is never really part of the 'Nation' " (Davila 2001, 87). This kind of marketing erases the ethnic diversity and the variety of cultural distinctions within the various Hispanic populations while it promotes negative stereotypes of Latinos as "poor" or "foreign."

Additionally, Davila (2001) affirms that ethnic marketing remains politicized and helps create the "good" ethnic consumer. Differences in class, generation, and gender are also often missing from the marketing, and Hispanic and Latino marketing is often reduced to notions of "culture" (85–86). A focus on culture often minimizes the importance of race or immigration. Davila asserts that "[e]thnic marketing in general—not solely Hispanic marketing—responds to and reflects the fears and anxieties of mainstream U.S. Society about its 'others,' thus reiterating the demands for an idealized, good, all-American citizenship in their constructed commercial images and discourses" (212). Both production and consumption interests are important as they highlight how corporations and marketers profit while also revealing how ethnic communities may use these products to create and express ethnic identities (2001). In the conclusion, I discuss how the production and consumption of social media allow Muslim women to express religious identities.

Shalani Shankar's (2008) work on Indian immigrant identity, youth culture, and consumption highlight the creation of the category "Desi." She argues that "[t]he emergence of the category 'Desi' is a significant moment for South Asian diaspora studies, for it signals a shift for South Asians as immigrants longing to return to a homeland to public consumers and producers of widely circulating cultural and linguistic forms" (4). Shankar expands on Veblen's and Bourdieu's arguments that objects are social markers that indicate social class (208), and further explains "[u]pper middle-class Desis have been able to take advantage of the model minority stereotype to settle into wealthier neighborhoods with whites and other Asian Americans and send their children to high performing schools. In doing so, they have furthered the expectation that the next generation of Desi teens will do the same" (12).

Additionally, Shankar creates the term "Desi bling" to refer to a combination of South Asian, Bollywood, and Western aesthetics that emphasizes status. This blending of a flashy Eastern and Western aesthetic still emphasizes that jewelry and clothing are coded with social status, but "Desi bling" expands to also include cars and electronics (Shankar 2008). These patterns of "Desi bling" appear among SAMA women in their creation of South Asian wardrobes, but also in their luxury accessories and in their selfies, which are publicly displayed online. Shankar (2008) and Srinivas (2006) both conducted important ethnographies of how Indian immigrants use consumption in different ways: while Shankar examined "Desi bling," among Desi youth in Silicon Valley, Srivinas (2006) researched how Desi mothers in Boston construct a narrative of anxiety as cosmopolitan immigrants working to maintain ethnic and immigrant identities. In addition to this narrative of anxiety, Desi Muslim immigrants also need to preserve or recreate immigrant Muslim identities, which they often do through consumption, food, and wardrobes. We can combine the concept the narrative of anxiety along with triple consciousness to better understand the role that consumption plays for South Asian immigrants. Consumption for SAMA women also overlaps with the patterns of consumption of Muslim Arab and African American women because of both their shared religious identities as Muslim and also their racial minority status.

Suad Khabeer's book, *Muslim Cool* (2016), is an ethnography of African American Muslim college students and young adults in Chicago. The text explores how African American Muslims have created and reclaimed their African American identities through the consumption of hip-hop music and the development of a political consciousness; Khabeer further examines how these practices are often appropriated by second-generation, middle-class South Asian Muslims. "Forged at the intersection of Islam and hip hop," Khabeer argues, "Muslim Cool is a way of being Muslim that draws on Blackness to contest two overlapping systems of racial norms: the ethnoreligious norms of Arab and South Asian U.S. American Muslim communities on the one hand, and White American normativity on the other" (2). Khabeer points out the increased economic opportunity and privilege that South Asian American Muslim women experience in relation to African American Muslim women. She explains how Pakistani middle-class Muslim American women in Chicago are able to culturally appropriate African American style in headscarves and clothing and also in music. Khabeer traces the American Muslim women's headscarf in the United States back to hip hop, slavery, and Black Islam (135). She writes, "The Pakistani girl who thought camouflage was cool had access to a set of class-based and cultural privileges—she was educated and suburban and had more cultural authenticity as Muslim" (4). Pakistani Americans' projections of cultural authenticity are not questioned by other Muslims in the American Muslim context because they are immigrant Muslims whose families have been Muslims for multiple generations. Rather than think American Muslim women who practice hijab are caught between the two cultures of America and Islam, Khabeer pushes scholars to recognize that these women are negotiating between two American cultures (135). Khabeer explains that "by examining the interactions and intersections among different groups of Muslims, I complicate not only the meanings of the practice of female modesty, but also the ways in which we understand this religious community, and the Unites States itself" (137). My own findings build on Khabeer's research and show that SAMA women incorporate aspects of Muslim Cool, Desi bling, and also modest fashion into their consumption practices through how they dress and how they present themselves in social media.

AUTHENTICITY, CONSUMPTION, AND NOSTALGIA: ETHNIC FOOD AND CULTURAL CLOTHING

Sociologists and other scholars have argued that authenticity is a social construction, which is shaped by class, culture, race, and social capital (Heldke

2003; Zukin 2004; Johnston and Baumann 2015). For immigrant groups, ethnic identities are often tied to understandings of authenticity. A collective identity shared by a group of people, such as ethnic or religious identity, can be maintained through consumption. Perceptions of how authentic a person's South Asian or Muslim identity appears are often discussed and judged by insiders based on the person's ethnic food, clothing, and media choices. In the diaspora, the preparation of the authentic food of one's parents' or grandparents' home and is often equated with an authentic ethnic identity. Ethnic wardrobes can also be markers of "authentic" identities.

Food and apparel can be important ways to create nostalgia and signal home, although immigrants often hold onto imaginary homelands. Homi Bhabha (1994) writes about how those occupying imaginary spaces often refer to places that no longer exist and to a myth of purity and homeland. Immigrants often long for a place that existed when their families immigrated (1994). For the participants in my research, this imaginary homeland refers to a time when their parents immigrated from India or Pakistan to the United States between 1965 and 1979. Though their parents immigrated as first-generation adults, the second-generation women in my study were born and raised in the United States. Their "memories" are largely shaped by their parents' experiences in India and Pakistan in the 1970s and 1980s when most of them immigrated and to a limited degree by their visits to their grandparents in subsequent decades.

Tulsi Srinivas (2006, 9) states, "Multiculturalism and cosmopolitanism create anxiety because they expose us to new ways of being in and seeing the world. In the contemporary world, large populations of people live in diasporas, in exile, in migration for all sorts of reasons, self-chosen or not. . . . As people are living abroad or away from what they consider their 'home culture,' the idea of 'homeland' becomes an important nucleus for nostalgic sentiment." For Indian immigrants in the diaspora in particular, this longing for home culture materializes in culinary consumption, but is also shown through clothing and wardrobes serving both as ethnic and religious symbols. In her literary analysis of South Asian diasporic fiction, Anita Mannur (2010) explores why food is often a central marker of ethnic identity and community: "More often than not food is situated in narratives about racial and ethnic identity as an intractable measure of cultural authenticity. Food is not only key to the representation of diasporic identities but also in the romanticization of gendered and ethnic identities via nostalgia and culinary nationalism" (3).

Srinivas (2006) underscores the significance of nostalgia, framing how South Asian immigrants use foodways to maintain and create identity. Preparing authentic food is one way that immigrants signal their ethnic identity to each other (Abarca 2006; Diner 2003; Gabaccia 1998). The consumption of ethnic wardrobes is also tied to authenticity as well as to social capital and economic resources. Chatteraman and Lennon (2007) examine the significance of ethnic identity on the consumption of cultural apparel. Clothing, like food, is often used to symbolize both ethnic identity and religious identity for immigrants, and the social and economic capital of immigrants is often linked to getting access to cultural wardrobes.

Consumer culture helps express ethnic identities for new immigrant communities in the context of a hegemonic white society. Both food and wardrobes are also shaped by evolving notions of authenticity in the diaspora. Religion, in addition to ethnic identity, is marked by consumption, especially for Muslim South Asian immigrants after 9/11 and the Muslim immigration ban in 2016. Wardrobes, like food, are a site where these identities materialize. For example, donning the hijab or dupatta represents religious modesty both inside and outside of the religious community; wearing gold Indian jewelry and glass bangles signals ethnic identity in the ethnic community; and luxury accessories such as Tory Burch shoes or Prada bags signify class status within the general community. Luxury accessories are valued by middle class immigrants and within the dominant white American culture.

GENERATIONAL DIFFERENCES: RENEGOTIATING IN THE SECOND AND THIRD GENERATION

Though not all Asian immigrants are middle class, this study focuses on South Asian middle-class (SAMA) women as an important segment of the "model minority." In contrast to our many stereotypes about minorities as problematic, the model minority myth imagines Asian Americans as a positive type of minority. South Asian immigrants are considered part of the model minority because they appear to be academically and financially successful and have largely seemed politically passive in comparison to Hispanic immigrants and other minorities (Rangaswamy 2000). Statistics on South Asian immigrants often obscure differences among the many people who are lumped into that category. For example, 12 percent of South Asians live in poverty.[2]

First-generation, middle-class Indian women who emigrated in the 1960s and 1970s were either skilled professionals or the spouses of engineers and physicians who immigrated as a result of the brain drain. The brain drain, which in Western countries attracted scientists and many professionals in the medical and engineering fields from South Asia and particularly India during a period between the mid-1960s and the 1980s. These women frequently came from families with domestic help in India and when they immigrated to the United States, they had to manage a household on their own, while raising children and often working outside the home. They more often outsourced cleaning over cooking. While they chose to keep control of the feeding of their families as a way to maintain ethnic identity as perceived authentic consumption, this sometimes included using packaged or "heat and eat" foodways (Srinivas 2006). The "heat and eat" meals were South Asian, and not American TV dinners. Patterns from the homeland often shape food consumption patterns such as using convenience food, as I discuss in chapter 1.

Cultural policing through proving Desi-ness to other South Asian immigrants in the community and passing ethnic food ways and clothing styles on to the next generation are both important reasons for SAMA women to maintain collective identities. Yet second-generation SAMA immigrants have diverse interpretations of authentic ethnic food and clothing. This can be contingent on regional, classed, religious, and generational differences. Authenticity is indicated through clothing such as the display and wearing of salwar kameez (loose tunics and pants), saris, dupattas (south Asian scarves), and jewelry. The cultural policing of ethnic clothing, like that of food, happens within families, communities, and religious sites. The ethnic wardrobes are often interpreted as authentic if they are purchased directly from South Asian owned boutiques in the diaspora (such as from Devon Avenue in Chicago), brought over by family members from India or Pakistan, or ordered online from a global website that is run by South Asian or Muslim women. The issue of modesty norms and ethnic wardrobes complicates questions surrounding identities and authenticity for SAMA women.

The women I interviewed told me that they often bought hijabs and scarves locally from Western retailers such as Macy's or ordered online from modest fashion sites such as Hautehijab. Unlike the women that I interviewed, I purchased the lengha that I wore to my wedding at a store on Devon Avenue, which is run by a Pakistani family (mentioned in the preface). In 2002, when I was married, online options for purchasing wedding lenghas were very few. All of the SAMA women that I interviewed explained that purchasing special occasion ethnic clothes from Devon was seen as a last resort because Devon shops had become tourist traps. In addition, for special occasions, SAMA women preferred to have custom-made salwar kameezes.

This research was driven by my desire to understand how access and religion, in addition to class, race, and gender, shape consumption patterns. For example, how are SAMA women as cosmopolitan immigrants able to negotiate their identities through consumption of food, wardrobes, and social media? And how do intersectionality and triple-consciousness help to frame how we understand consumption patterns for SAMA women in a post 9/11 society? These questions led me to study SAMA women as minorities maintaining ethnic and religious identities in the current political climate.

METHODOLOGY

My data for this project is based on interviews with SAMA women in the greater Chicago area and an analysis of lifestyle blogs and Instagram content aimed at South Asian women and American Muslims. I wanted to see how these populations represent their own consumption choices around food, body, and dress in their own words.

I recognize that I have insider and outsider status on multiple levels with this project. I am South Asian American (with a Pakistani mother and an Indian father), Muslim, second-generation, and bilingual. In addition, I lived in Chicago for five years, from 1998 to 2003, while I was completing my graduate degree. However, I am also an outsider, having lived outside of the Chicago South Asian immigrant community for more than ten years. My insider status helped me develop a certain amount of trust with the women I interviewed. It also makes me sensitive to the nuances of the lives of second-generation Desi Muslim women in American society. I strive to portray their responses accurately as I seek to reflect a more thorough and nuanced understanding of the lives of second-generation Desi Muslim women in American society, particularly within the Chicago South Asian immigrant community. Most of the women I spoke with lived in the suburbs of Schaumburg, Woodfield, Oakbrook, Naperville, Skokie, and Niles, Illinois. Similar to Selod's (2018, 26) research, I also found many of the South Asian Muslim Americans I interviewed lived in middle- and upper-class suburbs. They all identified as Pakistani or Indian immigrant professional Muslim women who were born and raised in the United States. I interviewed all the women in English though I am bilingual in Urdu and English. Even though interviews were in English, there were a few names of foods and comments made in Urdu or sometimes Arabic that I was able to translate.

I conducted interviews in homes, restaurants, coffee shops, schools, and mosques, depending on where each interviewee indicated she felt at ease. Many chose cafes, their homes, or places of employment. I took notes on socio-economic demographics, class, and religiosity as I conducted my research. All of the respondents for this study were United States citizens, Muslim women, and were between the ages of 26 and 49. They all had college degrees and identified as heterosexual.

I chose Chicago because it has the second largest Indian immigrant and third largest Pakistani population in the United States (Rangaswamy 2000; Pew 2018). Since 2000, their population has grown over 50 percent, and there are more than 200,000 South Asian immigrants in the greater Chicagoland area (Asian Americans Advancing Justice).[3] In addition, Chicago has several suburbs with substantial South Asian communities, which are all comprised of more than 10 percent South Asian Americans (South Asian American Policy & Research Institute). This large population has also been instrumental in the creation of South Asian community centers; mosques; full-time Islamic schools; Indian, Bangladeshi, and Pakistani restaurants; and Indian grocery stores and butcher shops with halal choices that cater to Muslims. Lastly, because the South Asian American community in Chicago is so large, ethnic and religious groups within it are diverse.

Though many middle-class Indians and Pakistanis who emigrated in the 1960s and 1970s have settled in suburbs, the shopping and restaurant sector within the city, located on Devon Avenue on the Northside of Chicago, continues to thrive. India Sari Palace was the first Indian shop to open on Devon in 1973 (Rangaswamy 2000). Within Chicago, Devon Avenue has been known as "Little India" since the 1990s. The street has Indian and Pakistani clothing stores, jewelers, Indian salons, halal butchers, food markets, grocery stores, dessert cafes, and restaurants. In 1991, a stretch of Devon was designated as Gandhi Marg (street) and another stretch as Mohammed Ali Jijnah Way. In addition, there is a mosque off of Devon as well as many prominent Islamic and cultural associations throughout the Chicago suburbs. The Muslim Community Center and Islamic Foundation in Skokie established, 1969, which has an adjoining school in Villa Park, established, 1974, were established decades ago (Rangaswamy 2000). Because of the proliferation and density of South Asian and Muslim immigrants in the Chicago metropolitan area, it is easy to access immigrant stores that sell ethnic clothing including saris, salwar kameezes or hijabs, or halal meat products in both the suburbs and the city. Focusing on one region such as Chicago helps us gain a more in-depth look at a vibrant and diverse South Asian American community.

LAYOUT OF THE BOOK

Each chapter of this book develops the thesis that consumption is shaped by gender, ethnicity, immigration, class, and often religion, race, or politics. Food is coded by class, gender, and culture and has been studied in sociology, history, and other social sciences as a significant topic for analysis and cultural meaning. Dress and fashion continue to be examined by scholars in feminist studies and sociology interested in status and social identities. Consumption and consumer culture are increasingly useful in examining representation, especially of marginalized groups.

I start by exploring food in chapter 1 because this is historically a significant way that immigrants in the United States hold on to collective identities (Gabaccia 1998; Zanoni 2018). Through understanding culinary consumption, we begin to understand how ethnic food is often recreated in the diaspora with the intention of preserving an understanding of the "authentic" food of an immigrant's homeland. "Authenticity" in food is a contested term and continues to evolve (Heldke 2003; Johnston and Baumann 2015). Debates over authenticity often shape how immigrants choose to maintain food in the diaspora. In addition, regionalism, gender, politics, and class shape not only what foods are cooked, but also what types of groceries are purchased. Buying halal, organic, or local are important themes that also shape provisioning or the consumption of food groceries. In the second chapter, I explore how Desi women's culinary consumption habits are shaped by class, ethnicity, gender, and religion. Culinary consumption for the SAMA woman takes material form in the search for authentic, middle-class, and ethnic foodways.

The second key mode of consumption I explore is the importance of wardrobes and clothing. For SAMA women, bicultural identities often call for bicultural wardrobes. Class, culture, and religion shape what they consume when they are entertaining within and outside the community. Ethnicity and gender also play important roles in shaping shopping and wardrobe choices, especially within the community. But SAMA women have a triple consciousness, especially as it relates to how they view themselves through a white and predominantly Christian society. Outside of community and religious events, all of the SAMA women I interviewed wear Western clothing including pants and jeans or tunic dresses with pants to work or school. Their luxury accessories, including bags and shoes, often signify conspicuous consumption inside the immigrant community; however, SAMA women dress modestly when they are attending events at the mosque (even those women who don't wear hijab wear at least dupattas or scarves at the mosque). The women also spoke about their need for ethnic clothing, including salwar kameezes or lenghas, to wear to cultural events such as Pakistani weddings or Eid dinners.

The discussion also raises questions about how politics frame consumption for SAMA women, especially under the Trump administration. My interviewees spoke about their awareness of the anxious political climate, especially for Muslim Americans. One Pakistani woman spoke about how she had stopped wearing the hijab in 2015 but still dressed modestly. Another Muslim Indian woman noted that she was aware of how people viewed her as oppressed when she wore hijab. None of the women explicitly spoke about how they stopped wearing hijab because of 9/11 or Trump, but they expressed concern and consciousness about this. This is where we can claim that SAMA women have a triple consciousness in understanding how they are perceived by the dominant categories.

The last mode of consumption I explore is social media, including Instagram and lifestyle blogs created by Muslim and South Asian (often Indian) women. This analysis is important because social media gives SAMA women a chance to create their own representations online, and virtual spaces are often places where they can challenge the stereotypes of Muslim women as oppressed or Asian women as model minority. Lifestyle blogs and Instagram accounts created by SAMA women highlight themes related to food, the body, modesty, fashion, and clothing, which often reinforces religious norms. But social media can also be a significant site of resistance; Instagram, especially is an ever-changing visual medium, and it continues to reflect new gendered and racialized symbols. The Instagram influencers I researched are from both the Muslim Arab and the South Asian diaspora, and they represent a cross-section of Muslim representation on Instagram, where the content they produce often contains coded political and religious messages. Muslim Arab influencers, in addition to Indian and Pakistani influencers, shape the consumption practices of SAMA women because of the similarities in culture, but also because of shared religious and middle-class statuses. The following chapters show that for SAMA women, foodways, bicultural wardrobes, and social media are much more than areas of consumption—they are also sites of adaptation, resistance, and community.

NOTES

1. Salwar kameez is often associated with Pakistan but is also a North Indian outfit that consists of a loose tunic and matching pants. Styles have changed with fashion trends over the years. Salwar kameezes have historically had a "Muslim" connotation. This is further discussed in chapter 3, as well as origins.
2. 2019, Pewresearch.org, Budiman, Cilluffo, Ruiz "Key Facts about Asian Origin Groups in the U.S."
3. Advancingjustic-aajc.org

Chapter 1

Beyond Authentic Curry and Halal Kebobs

Noor heads to the neighborhood Whole Foods then to Madina Market to pick up organic spinach for the aloo palak and halal chicken to make biryani.[1] *She will make a final stop at the Indian grocer to replenish her spice rack with garam masala. She doesn't usually go to all three stores every weekend—an American grocery store, a halal market, and an Indian ethnic shop, but Ramadan is coming up and she intends to host an iftar (breaking of the fast meal) and dinner on the first Saturday of the month.*

Provisioning, in addition to keeping lists of grocery items she needs, is only part of the invisible labor that Noor engages in to feed the family and maintain the household. She cooks mostly Indian dishes though she will make an "All American" dish on occasion. She now has an Instant Pot so is also experimenting with online curry recipes from Khana Pakana including chilis, stews, and other pressure-cooker recipes. The Instant Pot is good for experimenting with online curry recipes because traditional Indian recipes often require time in the layering of ingredients and therefore Indian food often tastes better days after it has been cooked. Using the pressure cooker setting on an Instant Pot allows hours of slow cooking to happen in much less time.

INTRODUCTION

Collective identity maintenance for South Asian immigrants occurs through food in at least three ways: Food culture, for Desi women is a means of creating and maintaining their "authentic" middle class identities through gendered activities that are also engaged with religious practices. The preparation of Desi meals, which in the diaspora includes Indian and Pakistani food, is an important practice that relies upon notions of authenticity to delineate membership, inclusion, and knowledge, all key factors of material practice as a cultural marker. In this chapter, I unpack the ways that Desi women's culinary consumption habits are shaped by class, ethnicity, gender, and religion. Culinary consumption for the Desi second-generation Muslim woman materializes in the search for authentic foodways, which involves food production and culinary consumption that navigates a relationship between class-coded ideas about taste and religion-informed rules.

Sociologists and historians have established that consumption has been an important way for American immigrants to maintain collective ethnic identity (Ewen 1985; Gabaccia 1998; Halter 2000; Diner 2003; Cinotto 2014). Historically, food and consumption have also helped maintain collective ethnic identity for many immigrant groups including Italian, Jewish, Irish, and more recently South Asian immigrants in the United States and Arab immigrants in Canada (Prosterman 1984; Gabaccia 1998; Vallianatos and Raine 2008; Diner 2003; Ray 2004; Cinotto 2014; Parasecoli 2014). Parasecoli summarizes: "Solidly rooted in modernity and in the global flows of goods, ideas, practices, capital, and people, the establishment of food heritage and traditions plays an important role for the imagination and the cultural capital of migrants, not to mention for their economic outlook as producers of appreciated consumer goods" (2014, 415).

Donna Gabaccia (1998) focuses on the businesses and commercial food production that Italian immigrants founded, which both helped them ensure that their communities would have access to familiar foods and introduced them to a larger consumer public for economic expansion. Hasia Diner (2003) shows the importance of food for Italian, Irish, and Jewish immigrants at the turn of the twentieth century. For Krishnendu Ray (2004), the Bengali immigrants he interviews also use food as an important avenue for collective ethnic identity as they adapt to the American context.

Helen Vallinatos and Kim Raine's (2008, 366) interviews with South Asian migrants to Canada explored how shopping at ethnic grocery stores connects shoppers to other immigrants, counteracting the anxieties and isolation associated with relocation prior to the existence of South Asian and Arabic grocery stores in Edmonton. Tastes of home are also shaped by the layout of these stores, what is presented as "Indian" or "South Asian" as Mankekar (2002) demonstrates of her ethnography of Indian grocery stores in San Francisco. Krishnendu Ray and Tulasi Srivinas (2012) also explore the role of culinary consumption for South Asian immigrants with attention to ethnic identity, racial hierarchies, and class. Like many other groups of immigrants, Desi women help maintain collective cultural and religious identities through family and friends in the American diaspora, although their methods vary based on generation, socioeconomics, and other class-based factors, as well as types of engagement with religious practices.

Throughout this research, I have built on the intersectional feminist work in food studies that I referenced in the introduction (Forson-Williams and Wilkerson 2011; Power et al. 2019). An understanding of intersectionality in food studies that includes race, class, and gender helps broaden our understanding of how intersectionality can be expanded to include religion, culture, and immigration in the contemporary context to examine the importance of food in studying these interlocking social factors. Forson-Williams and Wilkerson (2011, 11) explain that applying intersectionality to foodways helps reveal difference but also highlights advantages for the dominant groups.

The relationship between gender, class, and food production is often highlighted when considering intersectionality and food, particularly as it signals racial-ethnic group membership (Abarca 2006; Forson-Williams 2007). Among and across racial-ethnic groups, the consumption of organic food and luxury ingredients reflects middle-class socialization. Gender has also framed food work, especially within the immigrant family, and food work is often positioned as a form of choice; in other words, to "feed the family" over other domestic tasks, becomes both a way of "doing gender" and "doing class" (Zey and McIntosh 1989; Abarca 2006; Counihan 2004; Power et al. 2019). Although the gendering of culinary consumption often results in the patriarchal practice of women doing the domestic work, for many women there is also decision-making power and agency in these processes (Avakian 1997). Uma Narayan's (1997) understanding of transnational feminism and intersectionality further complicates this analysis.

Addressing South Asian culinary consumption specifically using transnational feminism to grapple with ethnic appetites, Narayan (1997) welcomes the practice of eating of other food cultures over a kind of "food parochialism." Narayan explains that she grew up in a Hindu family and community where strict dietary restrictions associated with caste, class, and religion often reinforced boundaries among groups, and that eating the food of "others" allows for more openness to diverse cultures, perhaps allowing for less xenophobia. Ultimately, Narayan emphasizes that Western eaters should not hesitate to eat ethnic cuisine, but they should be mindful of the social, political, and economic processes involved in the food they eat. Even in the west, these processes often involve a complex colonial history interwoven with power dynamics (183).

While we can see this as a version of the "gastropolitics" that Appadurai (1986) and others (Parasecoli 2014; DeSoucey 2016) have described in global contexts, it is important to consider how the definitions and experiences of culinary consumption and identity construction are shaped by the intersectional positions of the actors in question. In relation to the experiences of SAMA women in the United States, intersectional frameworks that include race, class, and gender are critical in unpacking specific transnational experiences (Purkayastha 2012). Further, by using food and food production as the material means for examining experience, we can see the significance of an intersectionality that includes religion in the contemporary and North American context.

My research on SAMA women show how they engage in competitive culinary consumption with their professional peers by keeping up with culinary trends in dominant American consumer culture. At the same time, it also engages them with the women in their ethno-religious communities by renegotiating an imagined authenticity in the diaspora through ethnic food ways, recipes, and culinary displays. Often cultural policing is a way that women surveil or censor each other. The purchasing and preparation of Pakistani or Indian dishes, the sharing of traditional family recipes, and the socialization of children to appreciate their ethnic food are all ways that culinary consumption plays a role in collective identity.

In my analysis, the intersectional frameworks help in two other important ways: one, by contextualizing SAMA consumption in relation to a larger culture of non-South Asian consumers who engage with "Indian food" by eating, writing, cooking, and talking about it, often through the lens of "appropriation" or "authenticity"; and two, by emphasizing religion as yet another key factor in the mix of race, class, and gender locations that affect people's experiences.

Despite the fact that it is not among the "top ethnic cuisines" in the US, Indian and South Asian food are more common across the country than is indicated by the presence of high-end restaurants (*Washington Post* 2015). Trader Joe's, Whole Foods, local food coops, and other supermarkets routinely carry frozen entrees that have signifiers of South Asian cuisine, from chutneys to palak paneer, samosas, and "butter chicken." In 2017 *Business Insider* reported that Indian food was "trending," with more nuance in consumer understanding of different geographic cuisines within the category (*Business Insider* 2017). In 2018, *Food Business News* claimed that "the time is right for authentic Indian food" (Berry 2018). Other food writers also attribute the rising interest in South Asian or Indian food to its affinity to various food wellness movements and dietary trends such as vegetarianism (Shah 2018).

As migrants claim identity through culinary consumption, they do so in a context that includes consumption of food culture by non-South Asians as well as South Asian (Muslim and non-Muslim) immigrants. Thus, while South Asian Muslim American women are engaged in creating or recreating cultural identity for themselves and their families through food, the larger (mostly white) population around them are incorporating, consuming, and assessing the "authenticity" of their "Desi" culture, a process that bell hooks called "eating the other" (hooks 1992). Philosopher Lisa Heldke famously described this practice as "food colonialism," whereby some white Westerners "eat ethnic" as a way to enhance their status or cultural capital (Heldke 2003). Restaurant owners and food vendors often have to address the meanings and symbolism attached to their cuisine by non-group members in order to attract a broader clientele (Chhabra et al., 2012) such that business success is often predicated on negotiated ideas about authenticity (Lu and Fine 2016). Ray (2012) has written about whether or not South Asian cuisines can reach the level of economic and cultural status that "other" national or "ethnic" foods have achieved. For many Asian foods, with the exception of Japanese, the ethnic succession that Ray describes in New York restaurants is often elusive or a product of some fusion/hybrid approach.

Religion frames food consumption, especially for Muslim South Asian American immigrants in a post-9/11 society. In *Halal Food: A History*, Febe Armanios and Bogac Ergene (2018), explain that the term "halal" (what is lawful and permissible to consume in Islam) in Islamic law can pertain to much more than food and drink. Maintaining halal dietary restrictions among American Muslims refers to avoiding pork and alcohol, and this can be different than maintaining zabiha. Halal refers to only eating what is permissible according to Hadith and the maintenance of zabiha refers to eating meat that has been slaughtered according to Islamic law (shariah) and blessed by imams (religious clerics). Dietary prescriptions regarding halal continued to change over time and as Islam spread globally (36). Armanios and Ergene point out that eating organic, as well as eating less meat has been tied to halal eating practices more recently among middle class Muslims. They also explore the debates among Islamic communities within North American and Europe about the relationship between ethical eating as a Muslim and current social movement that critique factory farming, advocate for animal welfare and support vegetarianism, sustainable, and organic consumption.

Maintaining halal or zabiha dietary restrictions regarding meat consumption can signal religion or religiosity for Muslim immigrants, and is a way of maintaining ethno-religious traditions, especially for those that are South Asian and from a minority background in their countries of origin, such as India. According to the Pew Research Center, 77 percent of Indians are Hindu and 18 percent are Muslim in India (Majumdar 2018). The majority of South Asian immigrants in the United States came from India, followed by Pakistan, and then Bangladesh. SAMA women who practice zabiha are not necessarily more religious than those who only maintain halal but tend to view food as a way to maintain religious as well as ethnic identity.

THE SOCIAL CONSTRUCTION OF AUTHENTICITY AND CULTURAL NOSTALGIA

Preparing "authentic" food is one way that immigrants signal their ethnic identity to each other. As Mannur (2009) explains, dislocation and nostalgia often materialize in food of imaginary homelands for Indian immigrants. This functions both among insiders as well as outsiders. For South Asian immigrants in the diaspora, the preparation of authentic food of your parents' home for other immigrant friends and family is often equated with an authentic identity. Questions about "authenticity" are often about group membership as much as the precise reproduction of recipes, culinary tastes, and regional dishes (Narayan 1997; Heldke 2003; Abarca 2004). The perceived authenticity of food is shaped by society's expectations, and these expectations are often tied to cultural capital and class-based paradigms of taste (Johnston and Baumann 2009). The definition, experience, and production of South Asian, Pakistani, and Indian food was complicated by the diaspora experience in Britain in the 1960s and 1970s and then in the United States in the 1970s and 1980s, and by how Pakistani food became perceived as a national cuisine after partition (Appadurai 1986; Narayan 1997; Fielding 2014). As Appadurai and other post-colonial scholars have explained, Pakistani food only became understood as a national food because of artificial borders after colonialism and the partition of India and Pakistan (Appadurai 1986; Narayan 1997). Additionally, the diaspora has moved South Asian foods, recipes, ingredients, and culinary styles into places and cultural sites that transform some but retain other aspects of the source; we see this in South Africa, the United Kingdom, and North America (Chatterji et al. 2013; Sengupta 2013; Jagganath 2017).

As Heldke (2003) also reminds us, specifically when we are discussing food that is eaten in public commercial settings, most ideas about "authenticity" are attached to foods that are deemed "ethnic," which is problematic because of who gets to define its dimensions. White middle-class consumers often become the judge of what is considered "ethnic" and then ultimately authentic. Heldke and Thomas (2014) explain, "Whatever is most not-me (most 'foreign') becomes, by definition, what is most representative of the Other" (6). Krishnendu Ray (2016) further examines how, in relation to fine dining, authenticity is socially constructed; it is understood in terms of foodways. He argues that authentic food, and ethnic food in particular, is shaped by ethnic and racial hierarchies, which affect how ethnic cuisine is consumed in public by white middle-class customers. Ray is focused heavily on high-end restaurant consumption, and he argues that the consumption of ethnic food is largely shaped by the extent to which the countries of origin are economically and politically (and sometimes racially) valued in the site of consumption. The consumption of ethnic food is largely shaped by how economically and politically valued its country of origin is by its would-be consumers. In the United States, both Mexican food and Indian Asian food are examples of culinary traditions that have not historically been valued as much by white middle-class diners as western European foods, specifically French and Italian (Ray 2018). Though Mexican food became popular in the United States by the 1980s and was featured in wildly successful food chains such as Taco Bell, the success of Mexican fine dining among white Americans has been uneven (Pilcher 2012; Ray 2018). It is important to note how these discussions of authenticity are filtered through social constructions of class, such that culinary knowledge of "other" cuisines is a form of cultural capital (Finn 2018). This public version of authenticity is often contrasted with how members of a group view authentic food in contexts outside the scrutiny of a dominant culture. Abarca (2006) most aptly complicates discussions of culinary authenticity in her discussion of Martha Stewart's tamales, culinary literature, and Mexican food:

> Claims of authenticity in ethnic cookbooks and restaurants demonstrate the ideological complexities embedded within the phrase "authentic ethnic food." Whether demanding or delivering authenticity regardless of its consequences as cultural appropriation, the essentialization of other's food practices, or acts of cultural resistance from within, the ultimate effect is the same. Insistence on authenticity stifles culinary *chistes* from taking place. (10)

Discussions of authenticity of ethnic food take place by insiders and outsiders, and Abarca complicates this analysis with her discussion of culinary *chistes* (Abarca 2004).

Johnston and Bauman (2009) use ethnic connection along with historical tradition, understandings of simplicity (or unprocessed food), and geography to explore how authenticity is socially constructed. The ways that foodies use the terms "authentic" and "ethnic" to assess different foods and who prepares them provide a significant lens for us to understand how food is valued. Ethnic foods are categorized as ethnic or exotic as dominant groups decide what food is exotic or foreign based on time and place (24). The ethnicity of the food's producers is also often seen as a dimension of authenticity (81). Therefore, it is often assumed that ethnic food should be created by the immigrant cook or foreign chef. For example, authentic Pakistani food can only be created by Pakistani immigrants, which reinforces the assumption that a person's ethnic background shapes how they are able to prepare ethnic food (81).

Food can also be an important way to create nostalgia and signal homelands, although immigrants often hold onto imaginary or romanticized understandings of home. Homi Bhabha (1994) writes about how those occupying imaginary spaces often refer to places that no longer exist because immigrants often long for a mythical place that existed at the time when their families immigrated. Helen Vallianatos and Kim Raine's (2008) research on South Asian and Arab immigrants in Canada found that, "immigrant women value their habitual cuisines, and through continuation of their culinary practices, evoke and connect with 'home' and all the sensory and emotional experiences that this conjures. Non-recent immigrants, however, appear more nostalgic, idealizing foodways and lifeways to a greater extent than recent arrivals to Canada" (373). For the participants in my research, this imaginary homeland refers to a time when their parents immigrated from India or Pakistan to the United States, between 1965 and 1979.

FOODWAYS AND GENERATIONAL DIFFERENCES

Immigrants have diverse interpretations of their own ethnic foods and this can be contingent on regional, classed, religious, and generational differences. Daniel Weller and David Turkon (2014) note that generational differences between Latino immigrants in upstate New York shape how they incorporate foodways into their identity construction. For Italian immigrants, migration has often meant a consolidation of regional food traditions into either new or amalgamated traditions (Cinotto 2014).

The women in my research frequently came from families with domestic help in India, and when they immigrated to the United States, they had to manage a household on their own, while raising children and often working outside the home. This is counter to what first generation immigrant women from other racial-ethnic groups experienced in the United States because of class and career differences (Counihan 2004; Cinotto 2014).

Economic power in the household allowed SAMA women to hire domestic help. In India (and Pakistan), even among lower middle-class families, servants are often the norm largely because having domestic help is a marker of status (Sharma 1986; Donner 2008). Sharma (1986) also affirms that middle- and upper-class women in India can choose how they manage households because of their access to servants. This is possible through very low wage domestic labor that is not regulated by the state.

Because of this, the first generation of South Asian, middle-class, professional immigrants quickly adapted to supplementing home cooking with convenience and prepared foods such as pre-mixed masalas, frozen Indian dinners, take-out, or catering for larger gatherings. Since the changes to the U.S. immigration policy in the late 1960s, which opened the door for more South Asian migration, there has been an increase in grocery stores that are owned by or catered to Indian and other South Asian immigrants. Patel Brothers, for example, has been in Chicago since 1974 and eventually expanded to Houston, New York, and other metropolitan areas (South Asian American Digital Archive[2]). Frozen Indian food also became commonplace by the late 1970s; for example, Deep Foods was created in 1977 in New Jersey and became available nationwide by the early 1980s (*New York Times* 2003). Since ethnic identity was more salient for the first generation of SAMA immigrants, creating semi-homemade dishes or using catering was part of how this group maintained their households and entertained. Frozen and prepared foods were easily available by the 1980s and 1990s in these metropolitan areas. In describing these generational differences, the daughters of the first generation, who are the focus here, spoke about how their mothers used frozen kebobs or samosas, and regularly used pre-mixed curry powders such as Shan Masala to make biryanis and tandoori meats.

Tulasi Srinivas (2006) explores the role of packaged foods as part of culinary consumption among cosmopolitan Indian women in Bangalore, India, and in Boston in the 1990s where she emphasizes that consumption was shaped by anxiety of loss: "Fueled by a 'narrative of anxiety' over 'authentic' food as mother made them, the act of eating is transformed into a performance of 'gastronostalgia' that attempts to create a cultural utopia of ethnic Indian-ness that is conceptually de-linked from the Indian nation state" (193). In the 1990s, packaged Indian food became symbolic of authentic Indian identity for cosmopolitan Indian women (207). Ultimately, Srinivas explains that, "[t]he anxiety of cosmopolitanism in the case of the Indian family appears to be centered on food consumption. Food provisioning and food consumption in South Asian families are couched in what I call 'narratives of anxiety'—who is eating, how much, and what they are eating—are questions laced with anxiety for South Asian parents" (15). Similar to the Indian women in Boston in the 1990s, SAMA women in Chicago in this past decade discussed how their mothers used package foods but unlike their mothers they attempted to cook from scratch.

These first-generation immigrant women did not worry about proving their "Desi-ness," as they were new arrivals to the United States, but rather often focused on maintaining a cultural connection to "home" through whatever culturally appropriate foods were available including packaged foods, while also managing careers. In this way, one could say that the first generation of SAMA women were perceived as South Asian first and American second.

By contrast, second-generation immigrants must prove they are Desi as they are often perceived as ABCD (American-Born Confused Desi), or fully assimilated and too Americanized (Maira 2002; Mannur 2009). Anita Mannur (2009) has explored why food is often a central marker of ethnic identity and community in her literary analysis of South Asian diaspora fiction. Food is one place that authenticity plays out in group identities among immigrants but varies by generation. At the same time, gendered expectations were salient among the people I interviewed; in the second generation, Pakistani and Indian women are often bicultural: American but also Desi. This multi-faceted experience shapes how class, ethnicity, immigration, and religion inform women's work of feeding the family.

Focusing on Muslim American women from South Asia allowed me to pull out some similar and different experiences in the navigation of the model, especially since religious beliefs interact with class as a way of making choices about taste and appropriateness in food procurement. Among the people I interviewed, there were many who were middle- to upper-middle-class professionals. While these women were not navigating the same issues of acculturation or cultural maintenance as first-generation women immigrants, it appears that they still held responsibility for practices that help maintain or create ethnic identity in their families, often through food practices. It varies, in that the creation of an American identity for these SAMA second-generation immigrants could be described as a renegotiation of gendered (and classed) identity through culinary consumption.

GENDER, CLASS, AND FEEDING THE SOUTH ASIAN MUSLIM AMERICAN FAMILY

Written in 1991, Marjorie DeVault's *Feeding the Family* remains foundational in understanding how food work in households is an active process that creates both gender and class performances for family members. Along with other sociologists of care work, DeVault outlined the important invisible gendered labor women often take on in feeding the family including making grocery lists, considering food aversions and preferences, shopping (provisioning), and preparing meals (1991). These tasks are part of "doing family" and are often ideologically reinforced through political and social emphasis on the significance of family meals for social cohesion, socialization of children, health, and well-being (DeVault 1991; Murcott 1995; Avakian 2005). Many of these studies center heavily on one demographic—often white, often heteronormative, and usually families with young children—although their insights have been documented among families of color, gay and lesbian families, and households across the life course (Beagan et al. 2015). In the ensuing decades since DeVault's study, gender continues to be an important theme in understanding food, and also food and the family (Carrington 1998; Counihan 2004; Williams-Forson 2006; Cairns and Johnston 2016; Julier 2013; Bowen et al. 2019).

Psyche Williams-Forson (2006) lays the groundwork for intersectional feminist food studies, using race, gender, and class in her ground-breaking work on black women, racist stereotypes, and food. Meredith Abarca (2006) examines Mexican women's home cooking to further complicate how class, race, gender, and immigrant history shape feeding the family, but also cooking as an act of agency. Kate Cairns and Josee Johnston (2016) highlight how middle-class mothering is tied to food and the family for Canadian families. Alice Julier (2013) emphasizes how class (and race, for African Americans) continues to intersect with gendered expectations shaping food in non-family contexts that are often lumped under the idea of "hospitality."

Returning to DeVault's (1991) research, she deftly connected questions of power to economic capacity, decision making, and deference in the family. For the white working-class families that she interviewed, just getting a meal on the table was the key factor. For those with more means, the meal is an accomplishment, where ideas about what is good food are enacted. While recognizing the fact that women are often the ones doing the labor of producing the meal, it is also equally salient to recognize how class, specifically as culinary capital, shapes food practices.

These women may outsource cleaning rather than cooking because they connect feeding their loved ones with their gendered and ethnic identities. In the second generation, South Asian immigrant women often keep control over cooking despite the ability to outsource it. The choice by South Asian middle-class immigrant women to maintain control of the food work in the household is often empowering and includes the possibility of emotional and creative fulfillment from feeding family or friends. The choice to cook for the family while hiring help for other kinds of domestic work is a gendered choice that Desi middle-class immigrant women make. As with many other middle-class women, preparation and consumption of food is also still linked to convenience, time, and money (Beagan et al. 2015; Cairns and Johnston 2015).

Recreating meals from traditional family recipes and from "scratch" resonates with Desi second-generation immigrant women in ways similar to that of other immigrants who have used food for the maintenance of their communities' ethnic identity, including Mexican, Italian Chinese (Theophano 2003; Abarca 2006; Counihan 2004). Though the first generation of Desi immigrants relied heavily on masala mixes from grocery stores, the second generation uses food as a way to recreate imagined homelands by making South Asian dishes from scratch. Although these foodways are not "public," that is eaten in commercial settings, there is a public component, where social events, community activities, and social gatherings in the home are a chance for Desi women to demonstrate their domestic culinary skills. In these settings, the cultural policing of women by other immigrant women in their own communities often results in inter-community surveillance. Women will often reinforce their understandings of authenticity within their own ethnic immigrant communities by suggesting the "correct" way to prepare an ethnic dish, offering alternative family recipes, or sharing regional ways of cooking. This cultural policing and surveillance are a result of community women wanting not only to prove their cultural, religious, and ethnic traditions in their new homelands, but wanting to mark their communities with cultural markers such as food and clothing. Therefore, they are susceptible to being seen as white-washed if they don't know how to create the Indian and Pakistani dishes of their immigrant heritage, but they are also trying to demonstrate their cultural capital in terms of foodie trends. Josee Johnston and Shymon Bauman's (2009) study of "foodies" does not focus on ethnic-racial or immigrant women, but it does explore how ideals about authentic food are filtered through gender and class-based practices, often in relation to abstracted class-based communities. Many of these women are "foodies," but their understandings of authenticity and exoticism are constructed within an ethnic immigrant community. For the women in this study, their ideas about authenticity and exoticism are constructed within actual ethnic immigrant communities.

Food rituals that maintain this idea of authenticity include family meals, festival foods, and feasting and fasting. In the Desi Muslim community, Eid dinners, iftar meals during Ramadan, and mosque potlucks are all rituals that help create community. In the diaspora there is less of a sense of regional cuisines than a sense of a national cuisine. For example, in their countries of origin, Indian and Pakistani cuisine was differentiated by particular regional cuisines such as Punjabi, Gujarati, or Hyderabradi; however, in the new country, they often become blurred into a national cuisine. Home food becomes one of the indicators of an authentic ethno-religious community that South Asian Muslim immigrants share. This is common amongst among many immigrants, including Italian and Mexican immigrants (Gabaccia 1998; Abarca 2006).

The food cultures that exist in multicultural societies like the United States continue to evolve with new flows of immigrants, power, politics, and resources. New waves of immigrants, xenophobia, and racism all shape food cultures. De Camargo Heck (2003) explains that food often takes on a more imagined authentic status in a foreign country because immigrants have such a strong need to maintain a traditional identity, and food is one of the ways immigrants are able to do this, though recipes and foods often change in the new country because of limited access to ingredients or technology (209–215). Although food helps immigrants maintain cultural identity, it is often altered in the immigration process. De Camargo Heck highlights how globalization plays an important role in the "pasteurizing," whitewashing, or watering down of global cuisine, and in the immigration process, food often undergoes adaptation to the host cuisine. She explains how "immigrants have preserved their food repertoire and adapted their recipes to the new ingredients found in the host country" (2003, 205). The adaptation of recipes that has historically occurred continues to be shaped by the dominant culture, but with globalization, changes in populations, and accessibility, we are seeing less adaptation and more resistance to homogenizing by the increased numbers of ethnic grocers and online ethnic markets. Many segments of post-1960s American immigrants use their food to help maintain their ethnic identities and resist cultural assimilation, particularly among Asian, Hispanic, and more recently Arab American immigrants: "[C]ulinary habits mark a strong resistance to a complete acculturation, so that old and new culinary habits are mixed and modified in ways that affect the cuisines of both immigrant families and indigenous groups" (De Camargo Heck 2003, 207).

Cuisines are not necessarily reproduced or maintained in their original forms. Recipes get passed on from generation to generation and are often adapted and distilled by interaction with new host cultures (De Camargo Heck 2003). In the new generation of SAMA immigrants, ethnic ingredients are easily accessible but may be substituted with items that may be perceived as more healthy, organic, or local. In my interviews, women discussed using kale instead of spinach for aloo palak, searching for organic and halal meat, and lastly visiting farmer's markets for local produce. Adaptations, substitutions, and hybrid foodways are also part of SAMA women's culinary traditions.

DISCUSSION OF FINDINGS: NEW THEMES IN FOOD, FAMILY, AND IMMIGRANTS

Building on Devault's work in *Feeding the Family*, I give attention to how SAMA women's relationship to feeding their families have been gendered and classed (DeVault 1991). Gender, ethnicity, class, and religion are all important in understanding the lives and food practices of SAMA women. Culture and religion are often intertwined and cannot easily be teased apart as important factors that shaped food practices for SAMA women. In the case of Pakistani food and Pakistani American women, culture is often synonymous with religion, for the women I spoke with were all South Asian Muslim Americans. Back in Pakistan, Pakistani food shared the dietary restrictions of Islamic law because pork and other forbidden foods were heavily restricted by the state. All the SAMA women spoke about observing Ramadan, and of some form of halal or zabiha food practices, either at home or outside the home. We could argue that this is akin to Jewish food traditions. Jewish food or Muslim food are material social constructions that have emerged out of ethno-religious cultures. Roger Horowitz (2016) explores this among the Kosher industry in the United States, and Liora Gvion (2012) examines Israeli food in Israel/Palestine.

Preparation and consumption of South Asian food creates a cultural marker which often includes ethnic and religious markers. Ethnic food helps maintain group cultural identity, and adherence to dietary restrictions helps maintain religious group identity. The consumption of organic food signals middle-class status, cultural capital, and education. A preference for organic food was a recurring theme in the interviews, and this was linked to education, class, and income.

Additionally, the choice to cook for the family while hiring help for other kinds of domestic work is a gendered choice that Desi middle-class immigrant women often make. As with many other middle-class women, preparation and consumption of food is also still linked to convenience, time, and money (Cairns and Johnston 2015). Although maintaining South Asian cuisine was important for these SAMA women, it also became clear that saving time and money mattered, even for upper- or upper-middle-class immigrant professionals. The factors of saving time and money shaped consumption practices of the respondents differently. Many of the women I interviewed were physicians or married to physicians, but other professions represented in the sample were educators, lawyers, pharmacists, teachers, dentists, and interior decorators. One 32-year-old woman talked about how money was a factor in buying groceries:

> So the supplies that give it to Mediterranean, I believe they are organic. . . . And then there are some like national brands that also are like certified organic, and this and that, . . . But sometimes it's more expensive. It depends, it depends on where you are and what the demand is, and things like that. . . .Yeah, and I believe Mediterranean is organic meat. And several other places may or may not be. I'm not sure about them. But Mediterranean is, is a little bit more expensive with their meat compared to the other places.

Time, money, and access all shape buying groceries and are part of feeding the immigrant family. Gender shapes who does provisioning, in addition to cooking.

ETHNIC MOTHERING, INVISIBLE LABOR, AND DOING GENDER

"Feeding the family" often remains women's work even when it includes picking up takeout, ordering semi-prepared meals, or heating leftovers on a weeknight. Arlie Hochschild and Anne Machung's (1989) work on gender and labor highlighted that the "second shift" is the extra labor that women perform at home including housekeeping, cooking, and cleaning after working a full day outside the home. This increased among white middle-class women in the United States by the 1980s, though many working-class women and women of color had been working a second shift historically (Hochschild and Machung 1989; DeVault 1991). Gender is displayed through food preparation, even amongst SAMA immigrant families where both parents are professionals. Desi women continue to work the "second shift," especially when it comes to cooking.

American middle-class Desi women in the second-generation often choose cooking over housework when it comes to outsourcing domestic labor, perhaps because cooking is more managerial and mental. In addition to cooking, they take part in additional invisible labor, such as keeping the dietary restrictions of family members in mind, keeping track of groceries that need replacement, and provisioning. For the women I interviewed, shopping often included weekly groceries, ethnic shopping, and *halal* meat shopping. Debates about healthy eating among the SAMA women in my research also included eating low carb, low fat, and low sugar foods. Samia chose to eat brown rice instead of white rice because she said it was healthier. Noor discussed eating rotis instead of naan because they were "lower carb," and she was trying to lose weight.

My interviews with SAMA women revealed that these mothers carry two burdens: to ensure their children have an affinity for home-made South Asian cuisine and to provide children with what they perceive as healthy or "good" food. Food work does not end with preparing authentic food. This invisible work often materializes as additional grocery shopping and provisioning as well as extra time in the kitchen and at the dinner table to ensure their children appreciate their ethnic heritage. Desi women often do this through family recipes, preparation of ethnic meals and the consumption of ethnic groceries. Laila, a 32-year-old Pakistani woman, discussed the many places she grocery shopped for halal meat and ethnic items. She explained:

> So generally, I shop once a week. And then there'll be meat shopping I probably do less. So like once every two weeks, yeah. . . . Grocery shopping, I usually do either from Aldi's or Trader Joe's. Um, and then some of the more ethnic products like halal meats and then like halal chicken tenders, stuff like that, like

I'll get from Mediterranean market. We also have a lot of halal options to choose from too, in Lombard.

Author: And then in addition to halal meat, are there any other specific things you have to get, besides Desi spices when you go to Mediterranean market?

Laila: So definitely Desi spices. My tea, I get usually get from there [Mediterranean market]. . . I usually get rotis, and porattas, naans, things like that, bread products that are like more, um, I get those. They actually have fresh porattas that are made by someone locally and they deliver it.

It was clear that Desi women often had to go to multiple grocers and markets to find ethnic and halal food items within the city limits of Chicago and in the Chicago-area suburbs. Shopping, in addition to cooking, often added additional labor and time to their weekly tasks.

The need to purchase Desi or ethnic groceries from ethnic markets was a prevalent theme in many of my interviews. But with the increase in immigrant populations, many of the women explained that they could find ethnic groceries in their suburbs and no longer had to go to Devon in the city. For example, Farah, a 35-year-old woman, expressed her concern about eating healthy, but also the need to purchase *halal* groceries and ethnic food. She explained her need for western cuts of meat as well as less familiar meat like goat:

So, we live in Lombard, which has been amazing cause everything is nearby. So there's two halal grocery stores I go to in Lombard, a Mediterranean Market, Madinah Market. Mediterranean is a lot nicer, and it's like, westernized, so like if I ask for like chuck roast they know what I'm talkin' about, if I ask for filet mignon, they cut it exactly how I want it. Madinah is Desi-owned. So I can go and get, I can get goat there, I can't get goat at Mediterranean. . . . So if I want like goat meat, if I want like, if I'm making *nihari* and we want tongue, (Laughs) we want something ethnic, we definitely find at Madinah. Madinah's cheaper also.

Farah's grocery shopping indicated a need for Desi food and halal meat. Her desire to cook nihari (a meat-based curry) and to shop for goat were both clear examples of Desi foodways. Her need for halal meat expressed her desire for religiously slaughtered meat. But lastly, her mention of filet mignon signaled her affinity to what she termed "Westernized." Many of the SAMA women strove to maintain religious, ethnic, and American identities through their foodways. Food practices are shaped by culture, religion, and class.

In addition to shopping for ethnic grocery products, women discussed children's preferences, aversions, and affinity to Desi food. The invisible labor that SAMA women often perform includes socialization of children. Several of the women spoke in detail about how they prepared food differently for their children.

After I asked her whether her kids eat everything, one 32-year-old Pakistani American woman responded: "They don't love to eat everything, but they will. Okay. They will, yeah, yeah. And I mean I've actually started cooking more blandly for their sake, 'cause my older son he doesn't like spicy food too much, so I've cooked more bland food than I usually would, so, for them."

Another woman talked about her toddler's preference for eating only pizza, and she tried to slowly introduce basmati rice at dinner. Another explained that her daughter was going through a chicken nugget phase, during which she was eating chicken nuggets at dinner, so she was trying to have her eat Desi food on the weekend at least when they were at community dinners.

Another Indian Muslim woman explained that though her children preferred American food, they would eat rice with dahl (spiced lentils):

> So I cook daily.... And they're usually Indian, like Pakistani food.... Where the kids... okay—maybe two to three times a week, something, and it's like American, which would be pasta, ... or like a grilled, you know grilled cheese. But that kind of cuisine. But other than that, they typically eat like rice and ... you know some meat with dahl or something.

A third married woman talked about her children's preferences for only Desi food:

> I used to cook every day, when I went back to work, um, what we'll do is I'll cook on like Thursdays or Fridays for the weekend.... We'll go out to eat here and there, but my kids primarily eat like Pakistani food.... They just won't eat like pizza, or they won't eat.... They won't even eat like—yeah. I think it's because I was home when they were born, ... and I was cooking every day.

The creation and consumption of South Asian or Desi food is not just about wanting to be the cook of the household but also about socializing children into appreciating or often preferring the food of their parents' origins. Mothers saw this as part of teaching their families to love their culture and have some ethnic pride. Women discussed how cooking for children often involved balancing the preferences of what they wanted to eat versus what parents wanted them to eat. This was often a negotiation between feeding children South Asian food versus non-South Asian food.

The preparation and consumption of ethnic/South Asian cuisine functions to help maintain ethnic identity for Pakistani families and the task to maintain and pass on cultural traditions is the task of women. Additionally, many middle-class women cook to meet their husbands' preferences (DeVault

1991; Cairns and Johnston 2015). Patriarchal norms shape domestic work, and for the families I interviewed, feeding the family was also gendered work. This gendered aspect of cooking is a prevalent theme, even beyond the immigrant household.

Roohi, another Pakistani American woman, explained the challenges she faced trying to find organic and halal meat because her husband particularly loved beef. Unique to Roohi's interview was that her husband cooked the red meat in her family. Though all the women that I interviewed did the majority of the cooking, this was one of the important exceptions where the husband did the cooking. The majority of the women that I spoke with maintained the food work if it involved cooking, ordering takeout, or organizing grocery-shopping. This was the one family in which the husband did the majority of the cooking, and he also bought the meat which made them an outlier in terms of gender norms. Naureen also discussed her husband and his preferences:

> I mean it, he, he, when they say like the, you know, way to his heart is through your stomach, like that's my husband. But so I mean, he'll eat Desi but it's definitely not his favorite. So, but, I'm sure I would be eating more, like even now I'm used to, I'm kinda like that, like if I go to my mom's house for a few days, and it's like Desi food, Desi food, but I need something different now.

Naureen explained that since her husband doesn't prefer South Asian cuisine, she would often end up having to prepare a larger variety of meals. As a result, she often cooked non-South Asian food to please him.

As DeVault (1991) demonstrated, many women take on the gendered expectation that cooking for the family must meet their husband's preferences. Deference to men's palates and needs as well as the timing of meals was a consistent issue among the women she interviewed. Twenty years after DeVault's original work, it often appears that patriarchal norms continue to shape domestic work, and this was confirmed by the families I interviewed. This gendered aspect of cooking is a prevalent theme, even beyond the immigrant household. Patriarchal norms often continue to shape the immigrant household, even in the diaspora where South Asian immigrants perceive society as less patriarchal. However, there was variation in the preferences of the husbands among the families in my study. Some husbands preferred Desi food and the women mentioned their mother-in-law's recipes and others mentioned preferences for all American food.

RELIGION, MUSLIM PRACTICES, AND FOOD

Food consumption and preparation are shaped by religious practices and dietary restrictions for many SAMA women. Through the maintenance of dietary restrictions and cooking of South Asian food, food is also shaped by religion or in this case Muslim identity. Maintaining halal practices can shape where you buy your groceries, where you go out to eat, and what you eat (Armanios and Ergene 2018). In Chicago, there is a growing market for halal grocery stores and restaurants. Until the 1980s, many of the halal markets and restaurants were relegated to Devon or "little India" in Chicago; since the 1990s they have spread to the suburbs, which are highly populated by middle-class South Asian immigrants (Rangaswamy 2000).

Food also takes on a unique religious significance, which is contingent on dietary restrictions including pork, alcohol, and meat preparation for SAMA women. Though some American Muslims do not maintain zabiha meat practices, a larger population maintains the restrictions of pork and alcohol (Center for Immigration Studies). In the second generation, we can observe how zabiha proscriptions are often discarded, but halal dietary restrictions of pork and alcohol are still maintained, at least inside the home. This was evident in the interviews I conducted. I found that even the Muslim Indian and Pakistani women I interviewed who were not observant, indicated that they did not drink alcohol or eat pork. It became clear that avoiding alcohol and pork were prevalent social norms in the SAMA middle-class community, at least among those who were married, had children, or were loosely tied through family or friends to a SAMA community. These social norms are a result of socialization within Muslim families and ethno-religious communities (Khan and Hermansen 2008; Armanios and Ergene 2018). Through my conversations with SAMA women and the formal interviews I conducted, I found three important typologies in terms of Islamic dietary restrictions. These three typologies included families who maintained zabiha practices inside and outside the home (the most observant); families who ate halal/zabiha meat inside the home but only practiced halal (avoiding pork and eating meat that is permissible) outside the home; and those that practiced only halal inside and outside the home (avoiding pork inside and outside the home). Respondents also indicated it was increasingly easy to find halal meat at restaurants that served zabiha products. It was also interesting that one respondent indicated that maintaining halal was more important than maintaining modesty practices. She explained that not all women who wear hijab are maintaining halal, and that eating only halal food is more significant religiously than wearing hijab. This was not necessarily a view that all SAMA women hold. Like Mir's (2014) research on modesty norms and hijab, there is also a spectrum of the observance of halal rules among South Asian Muslim Americans.

Halal was also often also discussed in relation to purchasing organic meat. For example, Junnah, a 31-year-old pharmacist, explained her concern about eating halal and organic:

> ...We do buy halal meat.. Me and my kids are halal only. My husband will eat anything. ... But in the house, it's only halal. ... We do, we go to Devon. ... I try places around here and I feel like the, like the meat's just not as good as like what you get from Devon. ... Um, I wanna say like every like two months maybe. ... I have a deep freezer, I just stuff it, and since I don't cook that often. ... So, we buy organic dairy. ... So I will buy . . . eggs and milk, always organic. I've been thinking of switching to organic chicken, um . . . just—like for the kids, especially my daughter, with the hormones, and like, like all that.

Purchasing organic groceries was often connected to feeding the family and maintaining zabiha was also closely related to feeding children. A 31-year-old teacher emphasized that everyone in her family eats exclusively zabiha and organic. Although neither she nor her husband grew up with zabiha, now that they have kids, they only eat zabiha.

In the families I interviewed, zabiha became more of the norm after these SAMA couples had children. Another woman I spoke with, Leena, a 33-year-old mother, shared that her family only ate zabiha because of the kids. The research on religiosity has shown that young adults become more religious after they have children and immigrants tend to be more religious than they were in their countries of origin (Ebaugh and Chafetz 2012). New immigrants tend to often display religiosity through outward indicators such as mosque attendance and rituals. Here Leena explains her choices:

> So, I grew up eating only zabiah at home. Okay. But we would eat outside meat if we were outside. My husband grew up, uh, he grew up in Chicago, so he grew up eating exclusively only zabiha, so he, it was a much bigger deal for him. So, when we got married, I transitioned to only eating zabiha. So I guess we both grew up only having zabiha in the house, but in terms of eating outside meat, now that we're married with kids, we only eat zabiha, even outside.

Another recurring theme that emerged in my data was how wanting *halal* meat was connected to wanting "clean" meat as a reference to safety or hygiene. Cleanliness seemed to be related to how the meat was packaged, processed or cleaned. A Pakistani American teacher, Khadija, explained:

> And there are many options for finding halal meat also besides Mediterranean market. ... Oh yeah. Mediterranean has it, Tandoor Express has it. There's

another one . . . it's also nearby; there's another one called Madina Market. And you know you kind of go to each one and you kinda feel it out, and like some of 'em actually have the same supplier, but then depending on how they store the meat, how they cut the meat, how they package it and stuff like that. Then, that's why I prefer Mediterranean cause it feels a little bit cleaner, a little bit more like professional for me.

Roohi also expressed her concern about buying halal and good quality meat, and she emphasized both freshness and cleanliness as an issue:

But to be honest, for me it's a pull between that and then how good quality the meat is. So, I tend a little more to the side of organic if I can. So, I don't have a problem with buying organic ground beef from Costco, because I know it's good quality, versus if I go to the Indian store, or the. . . um, halal store, I don't really know where that meat came from. What is it fed? Is it really halal? You know, all those questions. Is it sanitary in the, in the back of that store? So, I will tend for that. Um, for the chicken, I buy, uh, [zabiha], and that's from Fresh Farms. So, I don't go, I don't have a, I don't have an issue with like oh it has to be like slaughtered two minutes ago. To me as far as I can see, if the meat tastes really good, it's better than the halal you're buying for. so, who knows, maybe it's fresher. Um, and, you know, from talking to the butchers there, they assured me that this is as close to organic as you're gonna get without the organic sticker. So, you know, that makes me feel good about, yeah.

Having clean butcher shops as well as fresh meat was an overarching theme in the interviews. Overall, the respondents seemed concerned with maintaining dietary restrictions, but these practices were often shaped by also wanting organic meat, affordable meat, and "clean" packaging. Religion, in addition to class, clearly shaped the consumption of meat products.

The consumption of organic food in the context of "feeding the family" and especially feeding children is symbolic of "good" middle-class mothering. "Good mothering" is a social construction largely shaped by white middle-class Western norms, which are shaped by gendered expectations of mothering in the contemporary United States. Good mothering also shapes the parenting of Desi mothers in the American diaspora largely because of social media and friendship groups. But for Desi and Muslim mothers, organic can be tied to religious identity as much as middle-class identity as some of them interpret buying organic as being more ethical consumption when it comes to purchasing halal organic meat. "Good mothering" often becomes the dominant modeling of mothering for Desi middle-class women despite their own mothers' parenting styles, which are often viewed as outdated or politically incorrect. The consumption of organic food among middle-class mothers is linked with extreme mothering. "Extreme mothering" has further developed out of "good mothering" as middle-class mothers have turned their attention to organic, local, and homemade products and consumption practices. Research on extreme mothering emphasizes that feeding the organic child is a way that middle class mothers utilize ethical consumption to create distinct identities for their families (Cairns, Johnston, & MacKendrick 2013).

Many women, even those who were clearly upper class, did buy groceries and other products from popular discount big box chains such as Costco, Walmart, and Target instead of smaller grocery stores or Indian ethnic grocers on Devon, citing the value of saving. Trader Joe's and Whole Foods also came up numerous times as places that sold healthy alternatives with many organic and fresh options. Roohi, a 43-year-old Pakistani journalist and mother, emphasized her desire to buy organic food, placing particular importance on organic meat, dairy, and eggs. For her, buying organic was more important than buying halal:

> Um, dairy. All dairy, eggs, vegetables, fruits. Um . . . yogurt. I mean anything that . . . pretty much anything (Laughs) that I can get my hands on yeah. As much as possible, yeah, I try to get organic.

However, Deeba, a 31-year-old Pakistani woman, explained that it was important for her to purchase both organic and halal meat for her family:

> Yeah, so we, the family, um, we all eat zabiha, and we also eat organic. So, we'll just buy like the. . . . Crescent chicken. . . . And then the Creekstone Beef [another zabiha brand].
>
> Author: And where do you find crescent chicken in the Chicago suburbs?
>
> So, I just moved to Morton Grove like in October. . . .There's a grocery store that the manager's Muslim. So he says do all crescent and Creekstone. . . . Fresh Farm on Gulf has also organic. Um, chicken as well.

Nida, a 33-year-old woman, also indicated that eating organic was important, but could also be expensive. So cost and organic-grown items shaped her food choices. She explained:

> Yeah, we try and buy most of our fruit organic. Veggies we stick with regular for the most part. We're not too fad or big, uh, picky about that stuff. Other than that, we're not. . . . I mean we try to go organic, but if it's like double the cost, we definitely won't. But if it's close or it comparable I definitely will try to.

Similarly, Yasmeen also expressed an interest in eating organic but was equally concerned about expense. Even though she was financially comfortable, it was clear that purchasing organic seemed burdensome. She explained:

You know, I think, the families that I know, I think probably they can't afford it, because again it's pricey, right. Organic, I think everybody would like to buy organic if they can. But you know, $20 from Whole Foods gets you really nothing, and $20 at Mariano's will get you a lot more. So again it depends on your budget. For us, I think you know, I . . . I've always had organic milk in house for the kids from day one.

Afshan, a 35-year-old woman, explained her preference for Trader Joe's because of cost, cleanliness, and availability of organic items. I asked her why she chose Trader Joe's for her regular weekly groceries, and she answered:

Yeah, yeah. I mean cause it's organic, it's clean, you know, it's inexpensive compared to Whole Foods. Like, I think goin' to Whole Foods, and you know, I try to be, I wouldn't say I'm like 100% organic, but I try to do at least 50% in terms like meat and dairy. . . . Right, no, yeah, that's true, yeah. So, it's pretty, like it's relatively cheap, so that's why I go there. I often refer to Whole Foods as an "upscale" grocery store because it's known for selling a large amount of organic and specialty items.

Only one of the women I spoke to prioritized eating local food products, and she really focused on only buying local honey as it related to also buying organic products for her children. Tania explained:

Um, on a regular basis other than milk and eggs. Um, probably our cheeses [I buy organic]. Like the string cheese I give to the kids, yogurt, um, they like to have those little like slurpy squishy yogurt things the tubes, so those. Um. . . what else? Honey we try to get organic and kind of like a high-quality honey, but . . . So the suppliers that give it to Mediterranean, I, I believe they are organic. And then there are some like national brands that also are like certified organic, and this and that, yeah. . . .Yeah. Yeah and I believe Mediterranean is organic meat. And several other places may or may not be. I'm not sure about them. But Mediterranean is, is a little bit more expensive with their meat compared to the other places. . . . I do like to buy some things that are local, but I don't think that I'm like very aware of that. Yeah. I mean I do like to see oh, okay, this was, like the honey was local, you know.

Other food related themes absent in my conversations included gluten-free, vegan, and fair-trade, but buying organic, especially for children, was a dominant theme. The other theme that was absent in my data was sustainability. The mothers I interviewed did not express any concern about eating food or purchasing food that included sustainable farming practices. But one mother did explain that her children were concerned with the environment and they had encouraged her and her husband to start recycling before it was mandated. Sustainability as a broader theme was increasing in importance amongst the third generation, the children of my respondents. Three of the mothers I interviewed mentioned their children's interest in the environment, and recycling.

Overall, the most common food practice among this population was the consumption of organic groceries. Organic and upscale groceries signal class, wealth, and conspicuous consumption. The type of groceries a family has access to, can afford, and has the knowledge to purchase is clearly coded with class and cultural capital. As SAMA immigrants attain middle-class status, they adhere to middle-class consumption norms, which often include buying organic or what is interpreted as "healthy." Additionally, organic food can also be perceived as more ethical as Armanios and Ergene's (2018) research suggests. Therefore, organic meat consumption can be tied to both class and religion.

Desi Muslim immigrant women are able to use food to help maintain their ethnic and religious collective identity and to display their conspicuous consumption through classed understandings of food ways. Class, gender, and ethnic and religious status often materialize in the preparation of perceived authentic recipes, and frequently incorporate organic groceries and halal meat products. Food is an important way that collective identities are created and renegotiated in the diaspora. Interestingly, food can reinforce and reproduce hegemonic understandings of gender within the family.

CONCLUSION

Food traditions from South Asia are often recreated or even reimagined by new immigrants in the Western diaspora. This creative aspect of cooking for South Asian immigrant women is linked to reproducing recipes from their mothers and grandmothers and reinterpreting regional Indian or Pakistani dishes from cookbooks purchased in the diaspora. Heldke (2003) also emphasizes that colonized cultures maintain traditional food as a mode of resistance. Though hegemonic norms shape the production of ethnic food, immigrants can also resist this assimilation through the maintenance and reproduction of traditional food.

In the Diaspora, traditional food prepared with organic and upscale ingredients can simultaneously reinforce class inequalities and challenge culinary assimilation. The cooking and consumption of Indian and Pakistani food by SAMA women is a way to maintain South Asian identity and challenge the assumption that they will change their foodways to adapt to the dominant culture, but part of this adaptation includes the practice of buying middle-class ingredients, often organic or local. As new immigrants achieve middle- class status, they often adhere to middle-class shopping norms as they participate in the consumption of fair-trade, local, or organic products. However, by holding on to their traditional ethnic foodways, they maintain cultural and religious norms and pass them onto the next generation

Religion and ethnicity shape the foodways of SAMA women and also frame how SAMA women construct their wardrobes. The next chapter explores how fashion is also an important mode of analysis in exploring how religion, class, ethnicity, and gender shape consumption. In particular, the next section looks at how religion influences how SAMA women construct their wardrobes through modesty norms. Class and ethnicity also play a role in the construction of dual wardrobes for this minority. Returning to the narratives of anxiety that that Srinivas introduces for cosmopolitan Indians (2006), I argue that the narrative of anxiety is a framework for understanding the bicultural consumption and display of wardrobes, in addition to food, for South Asian Muslim American women.

NOTES

1. An earlier version of this chapter was published in 2019 in *Feminist Food Studies* (eds. Power et al.).

2. https://www.saada.org/

Chapter 2

Bicultural Identities, Prada Bags, and Saris?

Yasmeen is packing to head home for the last weekend of Ramadan and Eid. She just ordered her salwar kameez for Eid from Islamic Society of North America (ISNA), but realizes she also needs to dry clean her shift dress for her internship interview. The Eid outfit from ISNA is a long-sleeved silk shalwar kameez consisting of an embroidered loose tunic with loose pants and matching dupatta. Yasmeen ordered her black shift dress and leggings online from Zara. She knows that she can borrow dupattas or a hijab from her mother when she gets home. Her mother always has extra scarves for prayer at home or at the mosque.

This chapter takes a closer look at how South Asian Muslim American (SAMA) women in the greater Chicago area use wardrobes to construct ethno-religious identity and community. SAMA women negotiate collective identities through everyday and holiday clothing. For SAMA women, bicultural identities result in bicultural wardrobes, as exemplified by Yasmeen's packing list. For her internship in downtown Chicago, Yasmeen wears a loose, long-sleeved shift dress from Ann Taylor, which falls just above the knees, with leggings and a hair covering (hijab); but after work she will change into a salwar kameez before heading to an Iftar (breaking of the fast) dinner at the Islamic center in Skokie. Most of the salwar kameezes that she wears for Iftars during Ramadan are less ornate than what she would wear to a wedding are long sleeved, with salwar and matching dupattas.

Yasmeen was born and raised in the United States, but she maintains a Desi wardrobe as well as a collection of hijabs, but her Desi clothing gets worn infrequently—mostly at South Asian dinner parties and religious events. Her wardrobe reveals her multiple ethnic, religious, gendered, and class identities. Where she purchases her school and work clothes says something about her class, and what she wears to community dinners and religious celebrations says something about her ethno-religious identity. Community dinners include Desi dinner parties thrown by close family friends, such as first birthday parties (akikas), engagement parties, pre-wedding rituals (mendhis), Eid gatherings, and Iftar dinners during Ramadan.

Traditionally, a South Asian woman's salwar kameez consists of a loose-flowy tunic (kameez) with matching loose pants (salwar) and a long scarf (dupatta). There are many variations of salwar kameezes, and they come with short and long sleeves, in a variety of fabrics, and also evolve with fashion cycles. Silk, chiffon, and elaborate embroidery tend to be associated with weddings, holidays, and festivals. Pakistani wardrobes often function as both cultural (Desi) and Islamic (modest) wardrobes since salwar kameez are worn by both Indian and Pakistani women and are often modest as they always include long pants and a dupatta.

SAMA women, like other South Asian women in the diaspora, have agency in their consumption patterns (Bhachu 1995). Wardrobe plays a role in identity negotiation for South Asian immigrants as class and religion shape what they consume when they are entertaining within their South Asian Muslim community, while SAMA women adhere to Western middle-class norms in their office and school settings. Ethnicity and gender also both play important roles in shaping shopping and wardrobe choices, especially within the South Asian Muslim community. SAMA women are socialized to display femininity through both their Western and South Asian wardrobes via "acceptable" makeup, jewelry, and fashion choices. From a young age, Desi girls are exposed to South Asian jewelry such as mini hoop earrings and eye makeup, including kajla eyeliner. Since their ethnic identity is maintained through clothing (in addition to food), SAMA women often find themselves creating a second wardrobe. The South Asian woman's ethnic wardrobe consists of Indian or Pakistani saris, salwar kameezes and lenghas (blouse worn with an ornate long skirt). Maintenance of this ethnic wardrobe often requires time, economic resources, and social capital. Having the appropriate modest salwar kameez with a dupatta to wear to a Ramadan dinner party or a modern custom-made lengha to wear to a wedding is a way that gender, cultural identity, and class are all displayed.

Fashion, including clothing, reinforces class, ethnic, religious, and gendered identities. From wearing the in-season Tory Birch flats, J. Crew shift dresses, and Louis Vuitton bags at work to wearing the most on-trend saris, hijab, or salwar kameez fashions to the community Eid festival, mehndi party or wedding, cultural wardrobes are embedded with identities shaped by social codes and cultural capital. Insiders of an ethnic community will understand the display of cultural wardrobes differently than outsiders from the dominant groups. Wearing jeans and a sweater to an Eid festival would be seen as modest but would be against the social norms for SAMA women, who are expected to wear cultural garb that is festive and modest, such as salwar kameezes, to religious celebrations. Salwar kameezes and lenghas are both traditionally worn with ornate earrings and bangles. Indian and Pakistani jewelry is valued for its gold and stones but also for its cultural significance. Salwar kameezes and lenghas are both gendered and cultural clothing that are read by insiders of a community for their style, femininity, and modesty. A DuBoisian analysis of how consumption is shaped by ethnicity, culture, religion, gender, and class suggests that SAMA women possess a triple consciousness, viewing their minority identities through the hegemonic lens of white, patriarchal middle-class—and often Christian—society. SAMA women are racialized Asian minorities, women and often visibly Muslim.

According to Veblen (1899), items of material culture, including clothes, are social markers, and consumption is linked to status: "Consumption is evidence of wealth, and thus becomes honorific, and . . . failure to consume a mark of demerit," Veblen argues, dubbing consumption that aims to demonstrate one's economic position to observers "conspicuous consumption" (1899, 70). For South Asian Muslim immigrants in particular, clothing, accessories, and jewelry can all be analyzed as examples of conspicuous consumption. However, the wardrobes of SAMA women are not just shaped by a desire to signal status or wealth.

Bourdieu's (1984) analysis added cultural and social capital to economic capital by highlighting how knowledge and social networks shape consumption. In terms of SAMA women in particular, social capital through the Desi community and extended family plays an important role in gaining access to ethnic boutiques, clothing from abroad, and private home clothing sales. Research on ethnic and racial minorities also demonstrates how collective consumption and ethnicity are framed in growing immigrant populations (Davila 2001, Chin 2001).

Davila's (2001) research on Latinos in American society emphasizes the importance of cultural identities, ethnicity, and marketing for both political and societal reasons. Davila shows how ethnic marketing reinforces racial hierarchies within the American landscape. Davila also affirms that ethnic marketing remains politicized and helps create the "good" ethnic consumer: "After all, 'minorities' are obtaining the optimal, all-American right, that of being interpolated as consumers" (240). Similar to Davila's work, Chin's (2001) research on consumption and African American children emphasizes how race, class, and gender materialize through consumption, which is embedded in politics and social inequality (3). He argues that the "consumer sphere, by its very nature, is a medium for social inequality" (23).

As mentioned in chapter 1, Shalani Shankar's (2008) research on Desis in Silicon Valley also examines consumption, though her research turns to South Asian American youth. Shankar creates the term "desi bling" to refer to a combination of South Asian, Bollywood, and Western aesthetics that emphasizes status (80). This blending of an Eastern and Western flashy aesthetic still emphasizes jewelry and clothing as coded with social status, but "Desi bling" also included cars and electronics (Shankar 2008).

Research on fashion has illustrated that clothing is coded with both class status and gender (Davis 1992; Crane 2000). From blue jeans to little black Chanel dresses, the sociology of fashion has explored how class, gender, and sexuality are key elements of identity and fashion (Davis 1992). Blue jeans started as utilitarian clothing items and by the 1980s became fashion statements. Little black dresses were originally the uniforms of domestic help but were transformed into chic and high-status items by the 1960s (Davis 1992; Crane 2000). These wardrobe items have complex histories shaped by changes in social conditions for different socio-economic groups.

Though British anthropologists, including Daniel Miller (2005), have been engaged in close ethnographic research on collective consumption and ethnic identities for a few decades, there is a dearth of sociological literature on wardrobes and consumption by Pakistani and Muslim American immigrants.

Peterson and Kern (1996) explore how American taste amongst elites developed from highbrow to "cosmopolitan omnivorousness" by the 1990s. As "cosmopolitan omnivorousness" spread, snobbishness was no longer the indication of status. However, an openness to both elite (or high-brow) as well as more common (or low-brow) modes of consumption truly defined those with distinct tastes. SAMA women in my research also exhibit a type of high- to low-brow preference when it comes to clothing and shopping. These women have the cultural capital and economic resources to be omnivorous in their wardrobe choices, much like Michelle Obama, who may sport J.Crew accessories with a Tracy Reese designer dress or wear Banana Republic flats with a Tory Birch pant suit. They have the cultural knowledge about fashion and consumption and keep up with the trends at chain stores like J.Crew, Banana Republic, or Anthropologie but are also aware of high fashion from less known designers, like Clare Vivier, and more popular ones, like Stella McCartney. Ultimately, class privilege shapes the omnivorous choices these SAMA women make as they construct their wardrobes.

The consumption of fashion for SAMA women is not only coded by gender and class, but also shaped by ethno-religious identity. Bourdieu's (1984) analysis of consumption reveals how consumer goods signal status and taste. Using Bourdieu's understanding of taste and cultural capital, we can further develop how taste is a result of cultural capital that is passed on through families, ethnic communities, religious events, and Western society more generally.

Women learn to shop from their female friends, female relatives, and often their mothers. Through shopping together, they learn about new styles and brands but also transmit cultural capital about global and local fashion (Zukin

2004). They share information about the newest trends in salwar kameezes in Pakistan and saris in India, but also about changing lengths in blue jeans and designer bags in the United States. For SAMA women, these shopping bonds are friendship bonds, but they also reinforce ethnic bonds within the immigrant and religious community.

Taste is a result of socialization by one's social class (through family and education) and status learned through society. In the case of SAMA women, both middle-class American society and also ethno-religious communities contribute to their formation of cultural capital. Knowledge of social codes is key to displaying distinction within and outside the immigrant community, and for SAMA women there are social codes associated with ethnic wardrobes as well as with work clothing and luxury accessories.

Not only are their consumption patterns shaped by western tastemakers like Gwyneth Paltrow (some SAMA women follow Gwyneth Paltrow's Goop) or Beyoncé, but South Asian community members play a role in the cultural policing of appropriate wardrobe choices within their community, especially for religious holidays, weddings, and community dinners. What is culturally appropriate at work is not necessarily appropriate at community events. Ethnic clothing is more often worn in religious spaces and at cultural events. Modesty norms are also stricter at religious events, especially at mosques. Community surveillance of modesty practices is often shaped by a community's religious norms and expectations of women or ethnic expectations as women surveil the authenticity of each other's festival outfits. Cultural authenticity is often read through clothing items like saris, salwar kameez, and lenghas, usually made in India or Pakistan

Class, gender, ethnicity, and religion all shape the consumption of clothing and play a role in collective consumption for SAMA women. Salwar kameez varieties are shaped by class, ethnic region, and even modesty, lenghas are elaborate floor length skirts with matching blouses, saris also have regional, ethnic, and classed meanings. Designers, trends, quality, and fabric all shape how salwar kameez, lenghas, and saris are valued, but SAMA women who have higher cultural and social capital within the Desi community have access to a broader array of wardrobe choices. For example, more affluent women are more likely to travel overseas, to have salwar kameezes custom made, to have social connections in wealthier social circles where women bring back higher quality and more fashionable clothing, and are less likely to purchase clothing on Devon Avenue, Chicago's Little India.

Cultural capital is linked to social capital, and social capital is a direct result of who you know within an immigrant community. For example, being related to middle-class immigrants with strong ties overseas or marrying into a family with social connections enhances social networks. Additionally, religion pays a particularly important role in shaping clothing consumption for

South Asian Muslim women through the interpretation of modesty norms or hijab. Modesty norms may encompass hijab but are also applied to Western wardrobes and ethnic outfits. Muslim women who maintain modesty in their work wardrobes avoid low necklines, sleeveless outfits, and fitted fabrics. Yasmeen who wears hijab, mentioned how she only wore Western outfits to work, including loose shift dresses over pants or leggings and loose blouses with high necklines and wide-leg pants. She maintained a modern but modest wardrobe, avoiding see-through, tight, or short garments. Geography can also facilitate these kinds of choices in terms of access to Little Indias, like Devon, or ethnic stores and boutiques in the suburbs, though the internet has increased shopping options and made it easier to shop for global goods. Women's consumption practices are also enhanced through interaction with global economies (Bhachu 1995), which help reinforce bicultural identities through consumption.

DESI WARDROBES AND SOCIAL NETWORKS

I argue that SAMA women display their multiple identities through the lens of triple consciousness. This new understanding of the racialized American Muslim uses DuBois concept of "double consciousness" to frame the experience of the immigrant American Muslim.

Selod and Garner (2015) explain that DuBoisian double consciousness among Muslims is often used to minimize risk:

> DuBois's widely used concept of double consciousness (1903) has famously underpinned a whole stream of work on African-Americans' experiences in the USA. However, its basic premise, which is that minority groups learn to read themselves through the eyes and mindsets of the majority population, and regulate their behavior accordingly in specific contexts, is also more widely applicable. If anything emerges from the work here it is that all over the West, Muslims are deploying brands of "double consciousness" to manage the risks of discrimination, confrontation and abuse. (Selod and Garner 2015, 18).

By using DuBois's concept of double consciousness and expanding this framework to apply to American Muslim Asian immigrants, I suggest that SAMA women use a "triple consciousness" to construct their wardrobes in a white middle-class society aware of social codes shaped by race, class, gender, and religion.

In addition to class, race and ethnicity shape consumption. Culture is often tied to immigrant status, in that second-generation immigrants tend to be more assimilated into Western culture and aware of social codes and designer logos than their parents' generation. Immigrants are also more likely to hold on to "stuff because ethnic identity maintenance can be a reason to display ethnicity through consumption and in particular clothing. This stuff they carry from the homeland has meaning and often nostalgia" (Mani 2002, 117–136). Newer immigrants often come to the United States with fewer possessions and resources, and ultimately many may hold on to more and consume more than European immigrants who arrived much earlier. These additional items of ethnic clothing, ornate Indian jewelry, or silk saris carry signal capital in their own immigrant communities and are coded with regional and cultural meaning in the homeland and in the diaspora. For example, gold bangles purchased on trips back home to India or Pakistan after immigration to the United States are imbued with ethnic and classed meaning within the Pakistani immigrant community. Lenghas purchased for nikahs (weddings) locally, online, or abroad are valued not only for their material but for their intricate handiwork and often designer label. Wealthier families routinely travel back to Pakistan or India to shop for upcoming family weddings in Chicago.

SAMA women have a triple consciousness that shapes their ethnic, gendered, and religious identities. They are conscious of being American while being perceived as racialized and religious others. Their Muslim identity may take on physical displays of modesty, hijabs, dupattas, or even religious charms. SAMA women's triple consciousness heightens their awareness of how they meet shopping norms and negotiate their ethnic identities through their cultural wardrobes. A 34-year-old, Hina, explained how often she buys ethnic clothing:

> I try to get a new outfit for Eid every year. Usually if I get like two new outfits a year like, . . . I can wear it to a wedding. I don't spend a ton on my Desi clothes. I feel like—like I know some people who will, will spend easily $250, $300 per wedding—have matching outfit with their kids. . . . I probably am cheap when it comes to Desi clothes, 'cause it's just like I'm so used to my mom buying 'em for me and my mother-in-law buying for me . . . but it's like a lot of 'em are gifts . . . so I probably, I'm not into the desi fashion and that, I think because I'm not as . . . in touch with my Desi-ness. . . . I wear Desi clothes at weddings, when I go to my, my khalas' [aunts'] houses, or if I'm in Michigan—like you know for dinner parties where there's adults, and like weddings.

She further explained how cost is a factor, and since she still has relatives in Michigan, she often has easy access to purchasing affordable outfits.[1] She also emphasized how her Muslim identity is more important to her than her Desi identity. Additionally, Hina's explanation of how her Desi clothes are frequently acquired through gifts and sometimes also through online shops is not uncommon. Online shopping continued to be a recurring theme in my conversations related to acquiring a Desi or modest South Asian wardrobe. Hijabican, Hautehijab, and Modenesia were all mentioned in interviews as online sources for hijabs, modest clothing, and fashion advice. SAMA women explained that these online options were not only easily accessible but often more affordable than the options in the greater Chicago-land area. Farah explained her maintenance of an ethnic wardrobe relied on online sites for purchasing clothes, and that she was able to find a site through Facebook that directly sells clothing from the region of Punjab in Pakistan Even with shipping, it was less expensive for her to buy clothing online than locally from Devon she expanded. Online shopping continues to make it easier to locate and purchase ethnic clothing, especially salwar kameezes. The increase and variety in online ethnic and religious boutiques have created more variety and competitive pricing.

When I asked Farah how often she shops for Desi clothes, she explained, "I've actually completely stopped shopping for Desi clothes at the stores. . . . I found a lady on Facebook, . . . that I've been using for about four years now." When I asked where this seller lives, Farah responded:

> Gujranwala, Pakistan, so she's in Punjab. . . . Shipping is $25 for the first outfit, and then like $12 for every additional [one]. . . . But her prices are still, at, probably half of what I would pay in Devon. . . . [Before] one of my cousin's weddings four years ago, . . . my sister actually found her 'cause we wanted to get like matching outfits made. . . . And the price she quoted us was amazing for like a really fancy lengha outfit. . . . And I've been using her since then. . . . After I started using her regularly for about two years, about half of my friends and family have joined in.

Farah also explained that her friends have also begun to order online for Desi clothing, especially for weddings. The convenience of ordering online and the affordability of purchasing lenghas overseas both made this an attractive option. Though Chicago has a large South Asian business district, many SAMA women opt out of shopping locally and order ethnic clothing online or wait for relatives to bring back salwar kameez, lenghas, or saris from Pakistan or India. They prefer online shopping to local shopping for ethnic apparel because of cost, quality, and variety.

SAMA women who have strong South Asian family, friend, or community networks have better access to purchasing ethnic clothing directly from Pakistan or India, have better awareness of desi bazaars, and are more likely to receive clothing as gifts when friends or relatives go abroad. The social capital involved in having familial or strong immigrant peer networks is important because it enables the SAMA women who have strong social ties to have access to private shopping opportunities.

Cultural capital, social capital, and economic capital all play a role in maintaining the dual wardrobe. But SAMA women are also conscious of their bicultural identities in maintaining their ethnic identities through these wardrobes. Transnational consumption helps reinforce ethnic and religious online communities. In chapter 3, I explore the sites mentioned in the interviews, including Haute Hijab and Hijabican, which function as both fashion blogs and modest e-commerce sites.

CLASS, STATUS, AND CONSPICUOUS CONSUMPTION: BEYOND BOURDIEU AND VEBLEN

South Asian immigrant women have always occupied diverse positions in the class hierarchy (Bhachu 1995). SAMA women are not all middle and upper class, but a large percentage of second-generation Indian and Pakistani women are middle-class, largely because they are children of first-generation professionals that immigrated in the 1970s and 1980s with engineering and medical degrees. The women in this research were born and raised in the United States and were educated and socialized in largely middle-class environments. Most of these women are bicultural and are aware of status markers both within their ethnic communities and the larger American marketplace. Social media also plays a role in advertising and marketing to this upwardly mobile segment. This upper-middle-class, bicultural segment of American society has both the disposable income and the cultural capital to make discerning purchases that they see as good "taste."

SAMA women are also children of new immigrants, and when it comes to ethno-religious identification, consumption is a place where immigrants can display their ethnic identities. Unlike earlier immigrants, more recent immigrants convey their identities through what they purchased rather than what they inherited. Halter (2000) writes about ethnic identity and consumption. For immigrants in particular, the consumption of material goods became a way of signaling group and ethnic identities. Maintaining an ethnic wardrobe is one way that collective identities can be maintained for immigrant communities.

Ethnicity is often conveyed through ethnic wardrobes including salwar kameez, saris, and South Asian gold jewelry, while religious identity is displayed through interpretations of modesty. Though Veblen emphasized consumption's link to status, Weber emphasized consumption's link to hedonism (Weber 1958; Zukin and Maguire 2004). The history of Indian women's consumption of gold (often 22 karat), gemstone jewelry, and bright and silk clothing problematizes how Weber equated consumption negatively with overspending. In South Asian societies, bright colors, silk fabrics, and gold jewelry were often worn even by common folks as it was part of regional, caste, religious, and even ethnic identities in the host countries.

Upper-middle class identity is often signaled through luxury accessories. Shabana Mir's (2014) research on American Muslim college-aged women found that clothing is a significant aspect of how they display their classed identities: "Most Muslim American women participated in the intense and expensive fashion scene on college campuses. Dolce Gabana. . . . Banana Republic. . ." (88). In my interviews with SAMA women, class was often displayed through luxury accessories including bags, watches, sunglasses, and shoes. Several of the women I interviewed discussed the consumption of luxury accessories and designer labels. Emblems on bags and logos on glasses and shoes help overtly display designer and luxury brand names. One of my interviewees in Chicago spoke extensively about her consumption practices. Asra, a 46-year-old Pakistani American woman, talked at length about her love of designer bags, including Chanel. Though she went out of her way to explain that she buys bags because of the style, she then explained that Alexander McQueen was one of the designers that she does purchase.

South Asian practices including the consumption of Indian jewelry, South Asian ethnic clothing, and ornate accessories are linked to multiple cultural identities, rather than just social class or conspicuous consumption. These multiple cultural identities inform the triple consciousness of SAMA women.

DOING GENDER AND ETHNICITY: SAMA WOMEN AND THE DISPLAY OF FEMININITY

West and Zimmerman (1987) introduced the concept of "doing gender" as a social construction, where gender is an accomplishment achieved by being read as feminine or masculine. While "doing gender" is an active process, it happens in a context of accountability, where people's behaviors are policed or regulated if they stray too far from cultural norms and expectations. In response to social and cultural ideologies, men and women actively construct their presentation of self, which includes material aspects of their physical appearance including clothing, makeup, and accessories. These accoutrements are part of the performative aspects of gender, and while individualized, they are also contextualized and specific to time, culture, and place. Women construct their physical appearance including wardrobes, makeup, and accessories as part of "doing gender." SAMA women are often socialized into how they display gender through "feminine" clothing including Desi wardrobes and Western fashion. Building on West and Zimmerman (1987), Siraj's (2011, 196) study on British Muslim women also found that "appearance was central in the construction of femininity, through clothes, make-up, weight and sexuality." SAMA women "do gender" when they curate their Western and ethnic wardrobes, apply makeup, and put on accessories. Displays of gender and femininity are usually a result of socialization from the Western media, family, friends, and ethno-religious community.

Additionally, West and Fenstermaker (1997) consider other aspects of identity, such as race, ethnicity, and class, to be socially constructed according to how they intersect with gender. Mir's (2014) research found that gender, along with class and ethnicity, shapes how Muslim American women dressed on college campuses and that "feminine etiquette," along with class and cultural norms, shape how upwardly mobile immigrant Muslims are fashionable and modest (124). In terms of South Asian American women, femininity is largely associated with public displays of gender. From a young age, girls receive messages from mothers, sisters, and aunts in the community about how to dress, where to shop, and how their physical appearance will be judged by potential future spouses and in-laws. SAMA women are pressured to maintain an ethnic wardrobe for community, family, and religious events, while also maintaining a "work-to-weekend" wardrobe or one that includes both professional and casual everyday wardrobe pieces. These wardrobes are shaped by gender in addition to class and ethnicity.

For SAMA women, gender also intersects with religion in shaping women's wardrobes. Mir's (2014) research emphasizes that for American Muslim women the choice to wear or not to wear hijab on college campuses is shaped by race, femininity, and sexuality in addition to religion. Religion can materialize in multiple ways as a community marker, and for the women interviewed for this research, religion shaped wardrobes in the form of modesty. Modesty sometimes takes the form of hijab, but other times is interpreted as loose clothing, minimal makeup, or plain jewelry. Mir describes modesty practice as a continuum, with conservative or orthodox women wearing hijab on one end and those who are more liberal in their relationship to covering the hair on the other end. Mir explains this as believing in "the spirit of modesty, culturally or contextually interpreted" (89).

First popularized in northern India, then in Pakistan and in the Western diaspora, salwar kameez was often preferred over saris for the ethnic dress of South Asian Muslim women in Britain and the United States because of its modest appeal (Guha 2004; Hansen 2004). The salwar kameez and sari both originated in India, but since the salwar kameez was introduced by the Mughals, it has historically held a Muslim connotation. This connotation later dissipated when the salwar kameez was eventually adopted by many educational and other national institutions because it afforded women more physical mobility than they had when wearing saris (Guha 2004).

The salwar kameez was more common than the sari amongst the SAMA women I interviewed in Chicago, as well. Wearing long sleeves and loose

Western clothing was also a recurring theme in discussions of modesty. As Muslim women in the United States are increasing their presence on social media, we see a larger range of images of SAMA woman, especially on Instagram, as I discuss in the next chapter. But the multiple interpretations of modesty are not always represented in popular culture via televisions or film, as even in television shows like *ER*, Muslim women are represented wearing hijab.

MODESTY AND HIJAB IN THE UNITED STATES AND CANADA

Clothing is coded with religion via modesty norms, in addition to class and gender for SAMA women. Conforming to modesty norms is often one a way that SAMA women reveal their interpretation of Shariah (Islamic law) as it applies to dress. The verse from the Quran that discusses modesty has been loosely translated to mean women should not display their ornaments and should cover their bosoms (Quran 24:31). Though there has been some consensus historically by Imams that this refers to covering the women's hair, feminist scholars of Islamic studies have questioned this strict interpretation since the 1980s (Al-hibri 1982; Mernissi 1991).

Modesty practices among Muslim women vary in Muslim and non-Muslim societies. Since September 11, 2001, especially in the United States and in Western media, where Islam has become synonymous with fundamentalism and terrorism, the hijab continues to represent women's oppression. However, the reality of American Muslim women's lives challenges these limited understandings of women and religion. The SAMA women I spoke with have varied modesty practices that make use of multiple consumption projects including cosmetic makeup, jewelry, clothing, as well as hair covering.

Jen'nan Read's (2000) research on Muslim women in Texas suggests that for many, wearing the veil is a choice. Donning the hijab has generally been cited as common among observant U.S. Muslim women (Haddad 2007; Williams and Vashi 2007), but recent research from the Pew report on Muslim Americans claims that less than 50 percent of American Muslim women wear some form of the hijab (Pew Research Center 2007, 2017).

Furthermore, the vast literature on Muslim women, veiling, and the hijab has explored multiple reasons why women choose to wear hijab and challenges the earlier hegemonic arguments shaping debates about hijab, feminism, patriarchy, and oppression (Hermanssen 1991; Re'ad 2000; Mehmood 2005; Shirazi 2016). For instance, Saba Mehmood (2005) argues that Muslim women have agency and choose to veil for reasons of piety or to give them increased educational or work options.

For Muslim women who veil there are benefits and rewards, especially when living in a Muslim community, they may be "bargaining with patriarchy" (Kandiyoti 1988). Muslim women are able to move around more freely, attend university, and go to work when they wear hijab in their home countries. Muslim women in the United States may wear the hijab to symbolize their religious identity or express solidarity with the Muslim community (Khan 1998; Re'ad 2000). Leila Ahmed's (2012) work on the veil focused on Egypt initially but then turned to the United States, exploring hijab at the Islamic Society of North America (ISNA). She observed a decrease in modesty norms at the annual convention of ISNA even as women's presence in leadership roles and programming rose. These variations of modesty and hijab often have ideological, ethnic, or cultural differences mediated by class. Culture, class, nation of origin, and religious interpretation (as discussed in chapter 3) all shape how women interpret and practice modesty norms. As a result, race, class, religion, and sociopolitical status frame veiling practices in North America. Social status is just as significant in determining hijab wearing as theological interpretations of the veil.

Theological interpretation of the veil varies. Many Muslim women have interpreted hijab as covering just the hair; others have interpreted it as covering hair, neck, and ears; and others (such as the Muslim feminist scholars) have interpreted it not as covering the hair but rather as dressing modestly. In *Brand Islam*, Shirazi (2016, 144) explains that "because Islam is practiced across vast geographical areas with diverse cultures, languages, and histories, styles of clothing reflecting Islamic culture must and do vary significantly. Consequently, a question arises of whether there can be an appropriate, universal standard for Islamic fashion." There is great variation in how modesty is applied to fashion in reality. Modest Muslim fashion can range from wearing the traditional salwar kameez without makeup or jewelry to wardrobes that may not include hair covering to wearing a tunic with leggings. Because of its often-modest styles, the salwar kameez is commonly worn to both cultural events, such as dinner parties in the community, as well as to the religious events at the mosque. But a loose, long-sleeve dress over pants with a scarf could be worn to the mosque for prayers. Though a dress and pants would have no cultural meaning, it would read just as modest as a salwar kameez with a dupatta.

SAMA women who cover their hair either wear dupattas (the long scarves traditionally worn in Pakistan and South Asia), wear the traditional hijab (which covers their hair and neck but leave their faces uncovered), or wear the turban style hijab (which is traced to African styles and is sometimes worn by African American Muslims and younger American immigrant Muslim women). Among the women I interviewed, all who covered their hair wore the traditional style of hijab except for Zeenat, who wore the "turban" style of hijab, which covers the hair but leaves the neck and ears exposed. This American style of hijab was popularized by African Americans (Khabeer 2016). Zeenat had been part of Muslim Student Association during her college years and was socialized in a multi-racial American Muslim community, both of which influenced her interpretations of Islam and modesty. These variations in hijab and modesty practices are often more complicated than they might appear, as Khabeer (2016) documents in her work on religious authenticity among the hierarchy of immigrant Islam in Chicago. Khabeer's analysis of American Muslims in Chicago examines hijab or hoodjab as an authentic form of clothing consumption for African American Muslim women and finds that young SAMA women in Chicago often appropriate the hoodjabi styles of hijab. The hoodjab style shows the ears and neck but still covers the hair. It's been perceived as a hybrid of hijab and hoodies.

Fashion trends and religion both shape forms of modesty and hijab. Desi American Muslim women in the second generation that choose to wear hijab, cover their hair with hijab rather than dupattas. Desi Muslim women in the first generation that covered their hair wore a mix of dupattas and hijabs. For the Desi American Muslim women I interviewed, adopting the hijab was usually a result of religious socialization within the multi-racial American Muslim community, including involvement with the MSA (Muslim Student Association) and ISNA.

Throughout my interviews and informal conversations with SAMA, a three-part typology emerged to describe how religion shaped the consumption of fashion and wardrobe choices. Though it is somewhat problematic to categorize SAMA women's understanding of modesty solely based on physical displays, I opted to create the three categories: conservative dress, moderate dress, and liberal dress. Hijab represents a conservative interpretation of modesty. Women in this study who wore hijab all wore long-sleeved clothing and long skirts or pants. A second (or moderate) type includes women who do not wear hijab but dressed modesty, wearing only long-sleeved tops, long pants, and long skirts, and often minimal or no makeup and little jewelry. Finally, the loosest interpretation of modesty norms (liberal dress) was shown by women wearing short sleeves or sleeveless outfits that went below the knees. As with any typology, American Muslim women do not all neatly fit into one of the three types. More recently there are also newer Muslim immigrants who wear short sleeves with the hijab. But among second-generation SAMA women who wear the hijab, all see hijab as conservative interpretation of modest dressing. Among the women in my research, a range of modesty norms were practiced, from those women who wore hijab and long-sleeved clothing only, to those women who left their hair uncovered and wore sleeveless tops when they were not at mosques or prayer times. All the women I interviewed emphasized that they did not wear short skirts above the ankle as showing legs was viewed as immodest within the South Asian Muslim American community. Seema explained, "I sometimes wear sleeveless outside community functions, but I never wear short skirts." She added that she always dressed modestly at the mosque and at Pakistani dinner parties.

But applying these three types is not always so simple when we consider how modesty is applied to cosmetics, jewelry, or to tight-fitting clothing. Some of the women approved of light makeup and others spoke of ornate jewelry that would be worn to weddings or celebrations. Wearing makeup was a point of negotiation. Some women considered wearing heavy or bright makeup immodest. One woman spoke at length about how she wore more makeup when she wore hijab because she felt the focus was on her face. All of the women, including those who wore hijab, approved of eyeliner, or kajal. Their different opinions and choices reflect autonomy and agency in altering norms around modesty to fit their modern and active lifestyles.

Multiple interpretations of jewelry, makeup, and modesty norms reflect how SAMA women interpret and apply religious, cultural, classed, and gendered norms. Modesty can be interpreted literally in terms of "covering up," but it can also be understood as dressing plainly and avoiding makeup or jewelry. SAMA women exert some agency in constructing their own understandings of a "modest wardrobe." More recent research suggests that some women only wear hijab for part of their young adult lives, and many women continue to adhere to other modesty norms even if they don't wear hijab (Williams and Vashi 2007; Ternikar 2010). These findings challenge the ways that American Muslim women are often reduced to those who wear hijab and those who do not; instead, the practices of the women I interviewed point to the need for a more nuanced framework for understanding American Muslim women and their notions of modesty.

Accessories and makeup, as well as hijab and clothing are all important aspects of how SAMA women apply religious norms in the American context. The assemblage of various modesty objects and their relationships to one another help construct a modest wardrobe. Parveen, a teacher at an Islamic school in Chicago, explained why she didn't wear heavy makeup but found jewelry acceptable (emphasis added):

> We are required to do hijab at work. But I do hijab outside of this place [Islamic school], too. Um, it's so hard as it is to do hijab, if you wanna add a necklace or something, I don't think it's the end of the world. . . . Um, I'm not big on like heavy makeup though. I just feel like, you know, when they say that we're s'posed to not—you know, we don't want guys to stare at us. I don't think that a necklace is gonna do any of that, . . . but it's like heavy, heavy makeup with a hijab, or tighter fitting clothes, I don't agree. I just, you know, if you're gonna do hijab, you might as well do it correctly.

Similarly, Tanya-Diba, who also wore the hijab, spoke about trying to avoid wearing extravagant jewelry:

> I do think like whenever it crosses the line of being extravagant and things like that, and so, I mean I will wear jewelry whenever we're going to a wedding . . . you know. Either, like you know, poking the earrings out of my hijab, or like even having, you know, the tikka thing like on top of the hijab. . . . So I've done certain things. Or they have like the headband style jewelry on top of hijab—like that got really popular and caught on, and so, . . . if it's like a special occasion like that, I will, I will go ahead and wear jewelry. But on a daily basis, I really don't wear jewelry.

Where Tania-Diba spoke about avoiding extravagant jewelry, Zeenat spoke about needing to wear larger jewelry with the turban style of hijab. Zeenat noted that she wore larger jewelry, particularly earrings, but lighter makeup to offset the turban style of hijab that she wore instead of the traditional style that many of the other SAMA women wear (emphasis added):

> So, like, um . . . like with the hijab be—um, so I wear it mostly back. . ..so I wear it like a bun—like a turban, almost . . . and then there are other times I'll wear it normal [traditionally]. It accentuates your face. . . . So like, like what a would be a little bit of makeup on somebody else will look like it's like a pound of makeup on you. And so like that does play a role. . . . And then like jewelry-wise, so because I wear the turban style, I can wear like a necklace and earrings and stuff. . . . But with like the hijab, it's like, it's like I have to, I feel like I have to wear bigger earrings, because otherwise it's like, what, all throws off balance.

Zeenat chose to wear the turban style of hijab that was also reflected in Khabeer's (2016) research. This was an aesthetic choice she made because she viewed the turban style as more fashionable because it allowed her to wear accessories and jewelry, including earrings. The turban style of hijab is a hybrid of African American Islam as Khabeer pointed out (2016). As Zeenat shows us, modesty and fashion are not mutually exclusive.

A last significant interpretation of modesty through wardrobe choices was how modesty was reflected in designer clothing. Only one SAMA woman mentioned that wearing designer labels with visible logos was not a modest practice. She explained that covering her hair and the body was only part of modesty and that modest dressing included using some reasonable restraint when it came to showing off wealth through flashy jewelry or labels. But wearing ornate or heavy jewelry was often discussed as a cultural practice among SAMA women. Owning and wearing Indian and Pakistani jewelry in particular was linked to displaying ethnic identity, which often included large gold hoop or elaborate drop earrings, jeweled necklaces, and glass or gold bangles from South Asia.

Many of the SAMA women I spoke to explained that they wanted to dress modestly but also be fashionable. Afshan, a 35-year-old Pakistani woman, talked about going to H&M, ordering online, and shopping in boutiques. Afshan explained:

> For myself, um . . . I do, I do H&M a lot, and then I do . . you know, the Asos online? That's what, I do that. . . . And then there's a Turkish website that I found that has like modest clothes. . . . And it's called Modanasia Asia. I think H&M's pretty good. Like everything, everything's pretty like long and, you know long sleeves . . . and even if you buy the longer tunics that are sleeveless, you can always like pair it with a cardigan or whatever . . . I like Hijabican. And then I'll usually go to it now once a year. And even H&M has good like scarves that I use as hijabs.

I also asked her if she had any friends that were into designer hijabs. She replied:

> Like Chanel and that? No, [laughs]. . . . I think that's more like when I used to live in Dearborn. . . . I think there's more in Dearborn. . . . Dearborn has a big Lebanese population. . . . And they go—everyone, all the families—go back to Lebanon every summer it seems like. And then they see like their cousins or whatever wearing Chanel, or Louis Vuitton hijabs, or whatever.

Wearing designer hijabs appears to be reflective of transnational shopping patterns and class. Afshan explained that wearing hijab, covering the hair, and long-sleeved clothing were all important aspects of her practice of modesty. Access to online sites like Hijabican, which I examine in chapter 3, and shopping at global chains like H&M came up in multiple interviews, offering evidence of the hybrid shopping patterns of young SAMA women. Afshan was able to construct a modest wardrobe by shopping at a mix of global chains like H&M and Zara while also supporting online Muslim- and women-owned businesses like Modenesia and Hijabican. Her comments also reflected her experiences shopping in Dearborn, where there is a large Arab American population, when she explained that designer luxury hijabs appeared to be more common among Arab rather than South Asian Muslim American women. Her hybrid shopping patterns also reflected her bicultural wardrobe.

Other women that I spoke with also discussed modesty norms, online shopping, and ISNA. ISNA's annual conference was often hosted in Chicago and was mentioned as an opportunity to shop for hijabs and modest clothing. ISNA was initially founded in 1963 by MSA (Muslim Students Associations) on college campuses, and its annual conventions began when their headquarters were established in Indianapolis in the 1983. It's the largest Islamic organization in North America and has grown substantially in size since the 1980s, in part due to high profile Muslim guest speakers such as Muhammad Ali (http://www.isna.net/about/). In addition, she explained the significance of ISNA. The convention has an extensive bazaar that sells clothing, hijabs, books, and many other religious items.

A 34-year-old woman, Kaneez, explained that she often bought her hijabs at the ISNA convention or in Dearborn, Michigan. She mentioned the need to have lightweight hijabs that matched her clothing. I asked, "And then what about hijab? Where do you buy hijab?" She replied:

> I go to Dearborn a lot in Michigan. . . . My in-laws are in Michigan, I'd say my, vast majority of my selection is from there. I get a lot when I go to ISNA. And then here and there I'll go to Charming Charlie, Target, if there's something. Woodfield [Mall]. . . . But I've also bought hijabs from H&M, Old Navy. And that's more of a per outfit basis. . . . But, when I first started Hijab, I was in Michigan, and I went out and I bought like 50, like to start off with.

Kaneez's hijab collection consisted of scarves and hijabs that she had purchased at popular chain stores like Old Navy and Target as well as those she had found at specific boutiques in Dearborn, Michigan and at the annual ISNA convention. She explained that she had access to hijab and modest clothing because of her ability to travel to Dearborn frequently. There are many Middle Eastern and Muslim-owned businesses in Dearborn. Kaneez's social capital (through the community in Dearborn and ISNA), cultural capital (the knowledge of how to put together scarves from chains and Muslim-owned businesses), and economic capital (the resources to travel to Dearborn and ISNA) all shaped her access to a wide vary of scarves and hijabs.

Zarina, a 28-year-old Pakistani American woman, spoke about how modesty, culture, and identity shaped her wardrobe (emphasis added below).

> So, I wear full sleeves and three-quarter. But when I'm running . . . or working out, I'll wear half sleeves. . . . And it's the same for me when I was Hijabi [wore hijab]. But like, I think, um, in terms of clothing, I try to get that a little bit longer, a little bit looser. Certain trends I just love. Like the harem pants—the wide leg pants. They're super halal and very easy, and they've been around for years now. So, I love those and I'll, I'll go with those when I can, *'cause they help my like tryin' to be modest thing*. . . . Which sucks though because the price is lowest when it's probably on a [fast fashion] cycle of the clothing. But for me, I, because of my lack of ability to know for sure, about the sources of say, there's, they could be a, a fancy like, a more formal brand that's more, um, you know, that claim they're more *ethical*, but how do I know that? So because I

don't know it for sure, it doesn't mean any more to me than I would be shopping at H&M.

Zarina also explained that she no longer wore hijab but still maintained a modest wardrobe by wearing three-quarter sleeve tops. She wanted to maintain a fashionable but also modest wardrobe. Zarina discussed her interest in buying more ethically sourced clothing and avoiding brands that had been cited for sexism or cultural appropriation. She spoke in particular about American Apparel's sexist practices and called their ads "borderline pornography" and mentioned Urban Outfitter's cultural appropriation, including Native American necklaces, symbolic indigenous images, or traditional tribal patterns on textiles.

Kaneez spoke at length about her pride in her Desi wardrobe:

I love having Desi clothes in my closet. Because for me it feels like one of those—one of the things that we're holding on to. . . . So I love having Desi clothes. I love wearing them. They're very comfortable. . . . I also go to Pakistan enough to be able to have luxury of buying Desi clothes. . . . Whenever I go myself to Pakistan, like thank God the trend is like the readymade things. . . [I] do not have time [to] . . . deal with the darzi [tailor]. . . . So, when I came—I just went in April—and when I came back this time, I came back with like three or four outfits that I could wear to my friend's wedding and stuff. . . . [Desi] weddings is a main reason I need outfits. . . . So most of my Desi outfits are formal. . . . I don't wear Desi clothes at home. . . . Except sometimes on Fridays [for Jumah prayer] and sometimes in Ramadan. And that's more so just to have the feeling of like. . . . Yeah, that, that's the feeling I'll love, . . . so the association with the holiday. . . . So mine won't fit in my closet, so I'm taking some of my mom's closet, to put all my Desi clothes. . . . Salwar-kameez. . . . A lot of my favorite stores in Karachi are starting to ship worldwide and get online.

Kaneez expressed her "love" of her Desi clothing and explained that her Pakistani clothes were clothes that gave her a feeling of cultural and religious belonging and nostalgia as she spoke of her salwar kameezes. She explained their significance in relation to both Pakistani weddings (cultural events) but also for Friday prayer and the month of Ramadan (religious events). Kaneez was one of the respondents who spoke about having a second closet for her Desi wardrobe. She also explained that when she did wear hijab, it shaped her clothing choices. When she wore hijab she had a heightened awareness of how she was perceived as an immigrant Muslim woman, and that she often was referred to FOB (fresh off the boat) by people in her own SAMA community:

Yes. When I was wearing hijab, I would work twice as hard on any outfit, and I would work twice as hard to look presentable and professional. Uh, it was twice as hard. . . . Makeup I wore more when I, I never wore glasses with hijab, and now I wear 'em almost every day. . . . FOB-y,—that won't look FOB-y on the same exact outfit. . . . So a braid and glasses right now, like I'm in FOB. . . . I can wear harem pants now [that I am no longer wearing hijab] without looking like a FOB. . . . I can wear a long skirt now without looking like an Arab hijabi. . . . But personally I feel like I have to work less, less to . . . achieve the same look because of no hijab, which sucked.

The theme of makeup and hijab also came up in conversation. Kaneez described a conversation with her mother about hijab in which her mother explained why she shouldn't be wearing more makeup with hijab because hijab is meant to be about modesty:

Yes. . . . Yeah, and it's almost interesting and ironic because part of the whole hijab thing is to be like modest. . . . My favorite feature about myself is probably my hair. . . . [Mom's] like, "Well, why would I wear red lipstick or a lot of eyeliner, or mascara, when the whole point of hijab is being modest?" And I'm like, "That's a good point I can't argue with, so. . ."

Zarina also made a reference to how Arab Muslim women dress differently than South Asian American Muslim women:

The majority of friends—the, I mean as Muslim girls in the U.S. joke about, my, my cousins live in Bahrain and stuff, and we always joke about the girls there wearing the [hijab] but their eyes are so done up. But it's like [she laughs]. And, but, and for me it's my, like while I was wearing hijab, I actually have TED talk about one hijab . . . mostly it's about my experience. So I used the, during, pre hijab, during hijab, and post hijab, to talk about my identity, the identity and culture. And it was one year ago exactly, so Trump was in campaign season, and I, I referenced that affecting me as well.

Zarina's interview touched on many significant themes related to consumption, shopping, makeup, fashion, and modesty. She explained that the Trump administration affected her into becoming more aware of her Muslim identity.

In my final interview, Yasmin-Rakshu discussed why she stopped wearing the hijab:

I stopped wearing it January of last year—2015. So, I just, I think a lot of it has to do with the whole . . . image around Muslims in America. . . . That I just like, I realized . . . when I started wearing it, my focus was really like, well I wanna prove that Muslims are normal and that Muslims can be nice too, and stuff like that. . . . Um, which it is great, ... But, you know, I don't think, there's very few people who know me and don't know I'm Muslim anyway, . . . because I talk about it. . . . Whereas, with hijab, I think that there's, uh, an in—initial bias. And then you're trying to prove yourself the whole time. And so, I just felt like that was less effective way of doing dawah [spreading faith] than, than not.

As she continued, she explained her understanding of modesty. Even though she no longer wore hijab, she did wear modest clothing and at least three-quarter length sleeves to cover her arms. Her motivation for initially wearing hijab was spreading the message of Islam as she explains:

Um, to me modesty's also relative, right. So, if you're. . .on the beach and you're wearing a skirt, a long skirt and a top, then you are modest . . . in that case. . . . And so, in America, . . . where no one is wearing it [hijab] I don't know if that makes me more. . . . I don't wear anything less than, . . . you know maybe like three-quarter sleeves or, or pants. . . . Like I, when I started wearing it, my main purpose was to like invite people to Islam and like people and stuff like that. I mean like what is modesty anyways. Right, there's multiple interpretations. . . . People think modesty is hijab, and it's not really.

Yasmin-Rakshu also went on to discuss how she wore more makeup when she did wear hijab because she felt that she was compensating for covering her hair. This way of doing gender is a unique pattern for SAMA women negotiating gender norms. Covering the hair but wearing more makeup is a unique but an important pattern to understand how SAMA women may display and negotiate feminine gender norms between Muslim norms and American norms related to physical attraction. Yasmin-Rakshu explained that when she wore hijab, she felt like she had to wear makeup because then the focus was more on her face:

And, and you know the reason also is, I'll tell you, I, I felt like I had to wear makeup when I wore hijab too, just because, um . . . your hair's not showing. So the focus is on your face. And, if you look tired, you look even more like. And, and I never wanted to look like oppressed. [laughs] . . . I hate to say the fact that my, my natural face looked depressed, but like with all of it like hidden away, . . . I just didn't wanna come across like I'm tired or feel sorry for myself. [laughs]. . . Like I said, like always feeling like you have to overcompensate, you know. . . . So now my system with salwar kameez, a lot of it like my mother-in-law will bring when she goes to Pakistan and stuff. . . . But no—I realize, when you tell people to buy stuff for you, like it's, the [probability] of it being awesome is lower. . . . What I, what I find is more useful if there's an event coming up, and I need something to just go. Even if I end up spending like an extra hundred dollars on Devon [Avenue]. . . . I got what I needed, . . . I got what I like, . . . It fits well, I can get it altered. . . . And then I have an outfit I can wear a couple times, you know, so. . .

She explained that her mother-in-law bought her ethnic clothing, including salwar kameez, mostly overseas from Pakistan, but when she needed something immediately, she would shop at Devon in Chicago. When she spoke about purchasing her work clothing, she gave many examples of stores she shopped at, and also mentioned that she did not spend a lot of money on her work wardrobe and was content with popular chains like the Loft and Ann Taylor:

> [I buy clothes at] the Loft, Ann Taylor. I think Zara's like seriously overplayed, and a lot . . . too expensive for that. . . . Um, I don't spend a lot a money on a whole. . . . I, I think, uh, anybody can look good in expensive clothing. So if you can buy something that is cheap, and [laughs] make it look good, that's the real accomplishment. . . . I can't remember the last time I bought something full price. . . . That's definitely a Desi thing. . . . I think the online shopping habit is the worst thing you can do, because there's like online promo codes, which is really exciting. . . . That and then a lot of a times it doesn't fit well, a lot of a times the stuff that I'll find is final sale so what if I need to return it?

Yasmin-Rakshu discussed modesty, consumption, and minimalism, and had just read Marie Kondo's *The Life-Changing Magic of Tidying Up: The Japanese Art of Decluttering and Organizing* (2014). She discussed wanting to buy less, not buying clothes online, and various interpretations of modesty. This final interview made me reflect on how class, religion, immigrant status, gender, and culture all shape the consumption of clothing, but might also shape shopping less in the future generation. Though all the women in this study had dual wardrobes, Yasmin-Rakshu spoke about wanting to downsize her wardrobe.

CONCLUSION: BICULTURAL IDENTITIES AND CYBER WARDROBES

SAMA women consciously use their fashion choices to express their religion, ethnic, gendered, and classed identities. SAMA women express agency and autonomy in how they negotiate and construct their wardrobes. Though many of them were raised in American Muslim communities, women often explore an array of modest wardrobe fashion, from wearing hijab to taking off hijab to wearing loose clothing, to negotiation modesty norms. This chapter explored how we can better understand the ethnic apparel of immigrants as they acquire higher economic status and cultural capital. Even among second-generation SAMA women, there is variation in how modesty is interpreted, how status shapes consumption, and how cultural wardrobes are constructed via online shopping, global boutiques, or ethnic local stores. But this research emphasizes that religion matters even for SAMA who women who don't wear hijab. Modesty norms continue to evolve and are often shaped by culture and class.

This next chapter takes a closer look at how social media represents the bicultural identities of Muslim women through fashion blogs and Instagram. Fashion, faith, and food are all important ways that religious, cultural and classed identities materialize in social media. In particular, the internet is a place where we often see both the reinforcement of hegemonic norms as well as reinterpretation of cultural and gendered expectations. Through Instagram in particular, visual codes are embedded in race, class, gender, religion and sometimes politics.

NOTE

1. Dearborn, Michigan has a rich history of Arab and Muslim immigrants tracing back to 1916 with the Ford Motor company. The Detroit metropolitan area has more than 300,000 Arab Americans. Detroit and Dearborn Heights also have a booming economic sector, including Arab American shops, restaurants and other places of commerce that sell Islamic and Middle-Eastern clothing, goods and groceries. The American Arab Chamber of Commerce is also based in Dearborn. (Gold Steven 2002; Howell 2003).

Chapter 3

Haute Hijab, Brown Girl, and the Consumption of Social Media

Deeba grew up in a practicing Muslim American family in Chicago. Though her mother and older sister wear hijab, she tends to wear tops or dresses that cover her shoulders and arms, and clothing that is long enough to cover her knees and ankles. She also follows the latest trends by following Muslim fashion blogs and South Asian lifestyle sites as well as Instagram accounts. But dressing in modest and fashionable attire is important to her. She often orders clothes online from H&M, but also purchases scarves through niche virtual shopping sites linked to blogs like Hijabican and Haute Hijab.

This chapter provides an analysis of social media aimed at Desi (South Asian) and Muslim American Women that helps us understand the role of consumer culture in the negotiation of SAMA women's identity. With increased access to and literacy in social media, SAMA women are able to create more nuanced and diverse representations of what it means to be Desi, women, and Muslim, and their posts often challenge hegemonic representations of Muslim women. Social media continues to change so quickly that it is often difficult to assess how it influences marginalized communities, but online spaces like lifestyle blogs and Instagram continue to evolve as sites of consumption, community, and resistance.

I argue that through discussions of fashion and food, lifestyle blogs can help create online communities, reinforce cultural norms, and operate as spaces of resistance and sites of alternative commerce for marginalized women. Identity signaling through consumption is apparent in both blogs and Instagram. Like bloggers, Muslim Instagram influencers reinforce norms through visual representations of wardrobes, food, and travel, and often signal their ideas on politics and religion through these symbols.

I expand on the previous studies on Muslim women's representation in social media that narrowly defined Muslim women through hijab, to include

Muslim women who do not wear hijab but exemplify "modest" fashion. Less than 50 percent of American Muslim women wear the hijab, but those that do not cover their hair often adhere to some form of modesty norms (Pew 2017). This research helps challenge stereotypes about Muslim women in popular media while also examining how we study visual images.

The consumption of social media in addition to food and wardrobes reveals how class, race, gender, religion, and sometimes politics materialize in third space identities. These third space identities reflect diasporic communities of immigrants who are at least second or third generation, and who are now part of a hybrid culture (Bhabha 1994). Shehnaz Khan (1998) applies hybridity and third space identity to Muslim women in North America as post-colonial identities in diasporic spaces. These sites offer both reinforcement of norms in neo-liberal and capitalist spaces, while simultaneously serving as spaces of resistance in identity negotiations for SAMA women.

Cosmopolitanism among "Muslim women" has increasingly developed since 2003 in particular as global and online communities began to grow (Cooke 2007). As Miriam Cooke points out, "In other words, new media produce radical connectivity across the globe and foster a new kind of cosmopolitanism marked by religion. Cosmopolitanism is at once unifying and diverse because the more people identify with and connect to each other the more will their identities be hybrid and split among the multiple groups in which they act and want to belong" (Cooke 2007, 141).

Hegemonic notions of femininity are ultimately reinforced through consumption practices and may be interpreted as neo-liberal and post-feminist understandings of cosmopolitanism. This chapter builds on Baluch and Pramiyanti's work on Muslim women who wear hijab in Indonesia known as "hijabers." Their analysis reveals that "hijabers" on Instagram are post-feminist while also engaging in religious rhetoric through displays of consumption. Their agency and choices are mediated through their elite practices. Consumer culture and "attendant commoditization of Islam in Indonesia" help frame their choices and agency. find that changing digital culture and changes in Islamic communication are key to understanding Muslim women's "online performance on Instagram" (1). Their research concludes that hijabers use Instagram to establish themselves as "independent women" but also emphasize their high economic status. The hijabers share Instagram images of high-end restaurants, exotic food, and global travel, and they use these themes to emphasize their independence, which is largely framed through a middle-class capitalist understanding.

Peterson (2017, 257) adds, "Social media provide new public spaces for Muslim women to share their experiences, but these spaces are infused with postfeminist pressures for women to do constant self-work to scrutinize their bodies and interior selves and to consume products in a quest for perfection.

The Instagram images of Muslim fashion gurus illustrate these intersecting demands and ambivalences that are specific to Muslim women in the West." Muslim bloggers and Instagrammers often reinforce status hierarchies and hegemonic notions of femininity as physically attractive: "Additionally, the ideologies of post-feminism are represented by another type of visuality that promotes dominant codes of femininity; women should appear beautiful, perfect, successful, and positive. Muslim women are also under pressure to fulfill the visuality of modesty" (257).

In social media, we often see how class is highlighted through food and travel over ethnicity and immigration status, and gender is negotiated through the construction of wardrobes. Blogs and Instagram accounts allow for an array of ways to reconstruct ethnic, religious, and western identities around gender and class. Kavakci and Kraeplin (2016) explain, "The Internet offers unlimited opportunities for identity construction. . . we found that the digital realm allows for opportunities for multiple constructions of self and that each of our three subjects revealed both an Islamic religio-cultural identity and a fashionable Western identity, at times emphasizing one more than the other, at times combining the two in unorthodox ways" (14). The authors continue: "While most Muslim women wear modest clothes for the sole purpose of safekeeping their beauty as submission to God, it is evident that religious and cultural norms are challenged so much so that the representation of hijab is reoriented sociologically." (15).

New Muslim networks for women that are also forged online, are often gendered, classed, and varying in religious interpretations. Lifestyle blogs aimed at Muslim women in the diaspora are important because they tend to have racially diverse audiences but reinforce a dominant, often conservative, religious interpretation of gender norms in the American context. This negotiation of consumption is socially coded with gender, religion, ethnicity, class, and sometimes politics. As Muslim bloggers present themselves in brand-name modest clothing, couture hijab, or tailored outfits, their choices are symbolic markers, which suggest how they negotiate identity through the consumption of ethno-religious clothing. Instagram influencers use similar techniques but highlight the "glossy" aspects of wardrobes, often emphasizing luxury accessories, high-end clothing, jewelry, and makeup. Bloggers have more of an ability to have forums for discussions where Instagram influencers' interactions are left to visual cues in addition to likes or short comments under captions.

On the Muslim blogs in particular, food is a way to indicate religiosity but also healthy living and lifestyle. On Instagram, food is often a way to symbolize status and culinary capital. Fashion is similarly used to demonstrate both religiosity and class status in blogs and on Instagram. Political behavior is more muted in the blogs like Haute Hijab and Hijabican, but more apparent among the Instagram influencers, especially Maria Ali and Fatima Alia.

The bloggers and Instagrammers that I analyze represent a range in how they display modesty and religion through fashion and food. Muslim bloggers and modest microcelebrities display hybrid culture through their multiple ethnic, religious, and American identities, but also third space culture. The bloggers and influencers I chose to highlight are all engaged in hybrid cultures, often shaped by triple consciousness. Where previous studies on Islamic fashion or modest fashion have focused on women in hijab, this chapter expands on how cosmopolitan Muslim women represent themselves. Lewis (2013, 44) explains, "A new category of 'modest fashion' has emerged and become legitimized over the internet, operation through a mix of commerce and commentary that connects faith groups with each other and with the secular world. It functions simultaneously as a taste-making mechanism, an ideological category, and a marketing device."

Throughout the blogs and Instagram accounts, various terms refer to the head covering. Hijabi is a term that American Muslim immigrant women who wear hijab use to refer to themselves, as opposed to the term hijaber used in Indonesia, or hoodjabi created by African American Muslim women (Khabeer 2016). Hijabista, a term that is a cross between fashionista and hijabi, is often used to refer to influencers and microcelebrities who are fashionable and wear hijab (Waninger 2015).

Through a closer analysis of food, wardrobes, and travel on social blogs and Instagram, it is apparent that SAMA women share information and create loose communities built around hybrid consumption patterns. Additionally, Dubois's notion of "double-consciousness" helps center an intersectional analysis that looks closely at how ethnicity, religion, class, and gender are all important modes for understanding how social media shapes these consumer identities. Ultimately, this triple consciousness materializes in online media through how Muslim women negotiate their religious, classed, and gendered identities. For second and third generation immigrants, this often results in third space identities which is a hybrid identity formed often after immigration or displacement (Bhabha 1994). Third space identities are a result of multiple cultures melded together that aren't easily defined as bicultural.

CREATING LOOSE TIES WITH ONLINE COMMUNITIES

This research also adds to the work on Muslim bloggers in Germany and the UK that found that online sites help create community for Muslims, especially as they are further marginalized as second-generation immigrants.

American Muslim immigrants have some parallels with German and British Muslims, though they have varied histories and class statuses:

> Thus the parallel discursive arena of blogs allowed German Muslims bloggers to articulate complex identities that are different from those typically ascribed to them in the dominant public sphere, a result of being able to speak in their own voices, without interference or oppression from privileged sections of society . . . bloggers acknowledged that blogging had made it possible to connect with other—mostly second- and third-generation—Muslims who were grappling with similar challenges related to representation, identity, and integration in Germany. (Eckert and Chadha 2013, 930)

Similarly, Warren (2018) finds that social media helps create community among British Muslim women as they also are shaped by a history of marginalization: "A crucial function of these platforms is strengthening supra-national identification with the global *muslima,* or Muslim female community" (2).

Latoya Lee's (2017) work on Black women and blogs suggests that blogs can be places where Black women can work on dismantling oppressive dominant ideologies or sites of "affirmation and self-definition" (97). According to Lee, blogs can also be sites of networking and economic freedom, as well as independence and commerce.

Through the discussion of food and health, or fashion and modesty, SAMA women can become part of online communities via lifestyle blogs and Instagram. Earlier research suggested that the friends we have online are often very loose social ties or "consequential strangers," such as the people we friend on Facebook (Haythornwaite 2005). But these online communities on Muslim or South Asian blog sites create important virtual communities for women of color because they help construct collective networks built around racial, religious, and ethnic identity. They also often provide opportunities for online discussion, debate, advice, and counseling around religious and gendered norms. Muslim women in particular can communicate, consult one another, and offer feedback to each other on how to dress, where to buy, and why to purchase certain products that are modest online (Lewis 2013). Social media, therefore, can function to create online communities for SAMA women but can also reinforce hegemonic norms.

Norris (2004) suggests that online communities can take on an increased role for marginalized communities who might not have access in face-to-face connections with others who share their marginalized identities. I add to Norris's thesis that immigrant Muslim communities, because of their heightened and marginalized minority status, also benefit from these online communities. The narrative of anxiety further enhances the role of online communities for SAMA women. The changing political climate in the United States, first after 9/11 and then under the Trump administration, further fuels the narrative of anxiety for Muslim immigrants and this often results in an increased need for community (Selod 2018). Instagram and lifestyle blogs are sites where some of these negotiations take place, and therefore online communities take on an increased role of importance for Muslim women.

REINFORCING SOCIAL NORMS

Social norms for SAMA women are shaped by Muslim ideologies, the Desi community, and the more general western media. Diversity continues to be a challenge even in global social media. de Perthuis and Findlay's (2019) research found, "In this mass-media universe, there were occasional representations of an ethnically, racially, and physically diverse fashionable ideal, but their appearance in fashion magazines or on the catwalk was still dependent on decisions made by a controlling elite and, in the broader scheme of things, could be seen as tokenistic (17). Lewis (2015) addresses both the sizeism and racism within the Muslim community:

> As I have argued, it should not be surprising to discover that sizeism and racism is a fact of the Muslim modest fashion industry just as it is in the fashion industry per se. Noteworthy in the United States, as elsewhere in Muslim-minority contexts, is the response this triggers from Muslims within the industry and from Muslim consumers. . . . That this appeal to unity may disguise power imbalances between different Muslims has been noted, including an understanding of how differentials of national and ethnic heritage intersect with class privilege. Yet, the ideal of inclusion continues to drive brand strategies and marketing. (267)

Similarly, Dufy and Hund (2015) find that bloggers reinforce hegemonic norms around, femininity, gender and class.

Hegemonic social norms around beauty and the body are certainly reinforced online but online social media venues vary in how they represent religious norms. Peterson (2020) emphasizes that "[o]nline spaces allow women to develop the authority to determine how they will incorporate a pious subjectivity with Western neoliberal culture" (1210). Online sites aimed at Muslim women, like Hijabican or Haute Hijab, emphasize modesty while still attempting to be fashionable. Both of these Muslim sites feature only women in hijab, long clothes, and loose clothing. These online magazines are mindful of how they use images of people and the types of images they choose to display avoid revealing clothing. However, Muslim Girl presents a broader representation of American Muslim women and features women in hijab as well as Muslim women that do not wear hijab. In addition to clothing that is modest, makeup and jewelry are often a matter of discussion on these sites as well. With the invention of halal (Islamically permissible) nail polish for example, we can see how religious laws (Shariah) about clothing and makeup are often mediated through consumption. But the example of halal nail polish is also important in understanding how Muslim women themselves interpret halal clothing or makeup and then create products that adhere to Islamic law.

The ethnic/cultural sites such as Brown Girl emphasize a shared Desi (South Asian American) culture, including Bollywood movies (popular movies in the Indian movie industry), Desi wardrobes, and Hindi music. Also, they often focus on second generational conflict, gender and family, Indian culture, and debates within the Desi diaspora. In particular, there are discussions centered on balancing bicultural identities and maintaining South Asian culture.

SITES OF RESISTANCE

Through discussions of food and health, as well as fashion and the body, women can create resistance in online spaces. Online sites allow for debates around what is "good" food or "ethnic" food to what is modest or trendy fashion. These can be sites of negotiation and places where Muslim or South Asian women can challenge ethno-religious norms around gendered and cultural expectations. Middle-class Muslim American and South Asian American women in particular have cultural capital in that they are well informed on Islamic law, cultural knowledge, social media literacy, and consumption.

A closer analysis of two categories of blogs, ethnic/immigrant blogs aimed at Desi American women and religious blogs aimed at Muslim American women, demonstrates that social media for SAMA women facilitates conversations around food, the body, and fashion. Religious ideology, gender, and class shape conversations on food, fashion, and modesty norms on the Muslim blogs. Gender, race, and class frame discussions on food, dress, and the body on the Desi blogs. These blogs often reflect this knowledge even as American Muslim women may debate or discuss what is modest, what is appropriate, and what is halal in terms of consumption. These inquiries and new interpretations can often result in challenging traditional Islamic authority or interpretation.

Websites run by Desi women as opposed to Muslim women have different limitations and opportunities. Desi bloggers raise questions about racial and sexist stereotypes of South Asian women as they address colorism, sizeism, and even homophobia. Unconstrained by religious ideologies, ethnic/cultural sites created and maintained by South Asian American women continue to challenge and resist hegemonic norms.

ONLINE SITES OF CONSUMPTION

Lastly, lifestyle blogs play a role in consumption, and often present alternative consumption sites for buying modest clothing and exchanging information about food, fashion, and travel. These sites also play a role in a capitalist economy, nationally and globally. Even though lifestyle blogs are often used as sites of consumption and can reinforce hegemonic and gendered beauty standards, they are also sites of autonomy. Women make choices about consumption and make them with increasing options online. They may use these spaces to discover new food trends, cookbooks and recipes, or they may use them to shop for modest clothing including abayas or hijabs.

South Asian lifestyle blogs vary greatly, as this increasing upwardly mobile population has ethnic, religious, and class diversity. The blogs aimed at Muslim women often feature modest clothing and hijabs. The conversations around purchasing from chain stores has heightened as Macy's has a modesty department. Nike and Uniqlo, in collaboration with Muslim designers, also feature modest fashion. Middle-class SAMA women often struggle with deciding between global corporate retailers that represent modest or hijabi women like the Gap or Nike and acknowledging that these global corporations are absorbing global fashion trends, but that they themselves as Muslim women and entrepreneurs also profit from selling hijabs or modest fashion, which is evidenced in the reading. These decisions are shaped by their class identities and embedded in the understandings of modest high fashion and luxury hijab as we see in Haute Hijab. Patterns of high-brow shopping also frames Haute Hijab, as this site emphasizes designer hijabs and is further evidence of omnivorous consumption.

The ethnic lifestyle blogs aimed at the South Asian immigrant community vary in the type of ethnic identity or Desi-ness that they reinforce through fashion advice, political commentary, media, and recipes. In addition to Desi blogs, my interviews with SAMA women reveal that religious blogs aimed at Muslim women also play an important role in shaping the consumption patterns of SAMA women. As mentioned in chapter 2, interpretations of modesty vary widely amongst middle-class American Muslim women, and these are reflected in the variety of wardrobe choices, from wearing hijab and wearing loose clothing to wearing no makeup or jewelry.

On Haute Hijab and Hijabican, women are only shown in hijab; though, on Muslim Girl we see more variation in how hijab and modesty are interpreted. Muslim Girl features multiple variations of Muslim women in modest clothing, others in hijab and Western clothing, and sometimes Muslim women in jeans and sweaters. Muslim Girl allows for multiple interpretations of Islam and modesty, reflecting the diversity of its readers.

A CLOSER LOOK AT MUSLIM BLOGGERS AND MODEST INSTAGRAMMERS

Building on Alice Marwick's (2015, 147) methodology for studying Instagram, I chose to focus on static images rather than video. In addition to four blogs, I also examined the accounts of four Instagram influencers and analyzed visual images of Instagram posts as well as the comments under posts. The Instagrammers I examined represent a range of Muslim women, from those that wear hijab to those that claim a modest identity but choose not to cover. I also wanted ethnic diversity, so I intentionally chose at least one South Asian and one Middle Eastern Instagram microcelebrity who was part of the Western diaspora. I wanted to examine accounts that had at least ten thousand followers. The 2015 article "How to Make Money on Instagram" in the *Huffington Post* suggested that the average number of followers necessary to have a paid endorsement is five thousand (Alexandra Ma, *Huffington Post*, 2015). From those, I wanted to follow a handful accounts that were diverse across ethnic racial boundaries as well as in their expressions of faith. I focused on four Instagram accounts, three of Muslim immigrant women who wore hijab, and one of a Muslim immigrant woman who did not wear hijab. Key themes of modesty/religiosity, beauty, the body, food, and politics in the Instagram accounts that I found reinforced the themes from the blogs that I had examined.

I intentionally chose blogs that highlighted an array of Muslim women's voices, including Muslim Girl which emphasizes religious identity versus Brown Girl which examines ethnic immigrant identities. I also highlighted Haute Hijab and Hijabican because my respondents mentioned them and therefore I wanted to understand how they were linked. My method for the blog analysis focused on content analysis in the text, focusing on food and fashion as key modes of representation that reveal how class, gender, ethnicity, and religion shape diasporic identities. Through this analysis, the theme of heteronormativity also surfaced on the hijabi blogs. I focus on fashion, food, and landscapes in these sites.

AMERICAN MUSLIM BLOGGERS

Blogs created by Muslim American women are often shaped by traditional gender norms and a shared understanding of "Islamic" culture. Reina Lewis (2013, 43) explores the intersection between faith and fashion, as she explains that the internet and online businesses are significant in terms of how modest fashion has grown. American Muslim blogs carry with them ideological and normative prescriptions of how to dress, and sometimes what to eat (halal or healthy).

Commentary and community are key themes in the online commerce aimed at modest fashion and Muslim women. Analise Moors (2015) emphasizes that online Islamic fashion has become so successful because of the growth of Islamic fashion within Muslim communities and online platforms. Like transnational travel, social media and e-commerce have facilitated access to modest options. Desi women who wear hijab or who adhere to religious modesty norms were increasingly likely to become hybrid shoppers and order modest fashion online, but still likely to make some hijab or scarf purchases at chain stores like H&M or Macy's.

In these sites, we can observe the creation of online communities, while also observing how Muslim women exchange ideas and debate consumption options. Muslim blogs aimed at Muslim American women are distinct from the blogs aimed at South Asian women because they carry with them the weight of being "Muslim" in American society. Muslim Girl and Haute Hijab are important examples of lifestyle blogs aimed at Muslim women in the Western diaspora. Some of the blogs like Hijabican are narrowly targeting women who wear hijab or might want to wear hijab. The name Hijabican was created for this blog to refer to American Muslim women who wear hijab in a Western context. She is "An American Muslim woman who wears hijab who chooses to embrace her culture without compromising her faith. Hijab + American = Hijabican," the author explains.

In my interviews with the SAMA women, they all spoke about modesty. Junnah talked about how she only wore long sleeves. Diba explained that she never wore skirts above the ankles. Yasmin explained that since she wore hijab, she only wore long sleeves and loose clothing. Social media, including blogs and Instagram, become gendered locations where women can guide each other and become religious authorities as they interpret and apply religious laws. Some of the sites aimed at Muslim women like Haute Hijab and Hijabican create alternative interpretations of what modesty means with discussions on makeup, jewelry, or clothing. Historically, the male interpretation of Islamic law guided how modesty was interpreted in Muslim majority nations and in predominantly Muslim communities. Online media has also increased American Muslim women's visibility in the discussions of modesty, fashion and politics. Through the success of sites like Muslim Girl and Hijabican, Muslim women are able to advise, inform, and negotiate how fashion style and modesty both shape their consumption practices and shopping choices.

HIJABICAN

Hijabican and Haute Hijab are two popular websites created by American Muslim women that are also sites of online commerce, which sell hijabs and modest clothing. Hijabican is a blog and online boutique catering to Muslim female readers who wear hijab. The site states, "At Hijabican, we believe a hijabi can. We are more than a fashion house. We want to empower and inspire hijabis to follow their dreams." Hijabican emphasizes the challenges facing American women who wear hijab in the United States. On this site, the authors emphasize that hijab is also associated with female empowerment as they explain "we want to empower and inspire hijabis." The site further defines Hijabican:

> Someone who believes that the hijab doesn't oppress a woman, but in fact liberates a woman and gives her the freedom to achieve her dreams whether it's becoming an astronaut to being a full-time home maker. . . . Because a hijabi . . . *can.*"

Dressing modestly and wearing hijab are presented as part of one's duty and faith in serving Allah (God) throughout this site. The website goes on to explain, "At the end of the day, clothing is a means of serving Allah by modestly covering our bodies."

The authors of this site emphasize that there are alternative consumption sites for purchasing modest clothing rather than buying from national or global chains. Since these websites were created, Macy, Nike, and Gap have featured "modest" clothing in their advertisements as well as in their stores. When images are used on the Hijabican site, women are pictured wearing hijab and long sleeved-clothing, long skirts, or long flowing dresses or pants.

Hijabican also offers features on personal training, body building, and exemplary women who wear hijab. For example, in 2013, they featured an interview with a personal trainer who explained:

> After reading a magazine article about calories in vs calories out I started running to lose weight. That really began my fitness journey. I saw how exercise and running particularly could help me maintain my weight and how great I felt

during and after I ran, and I was hooked. I stayed pretty fit up until I had my first child and had complications during my pregnancy that ballooned my weight to almost 200lbs. (January 12, 2013)

This excerpt is a representative example of how on these sites we also still see thinness and hijabed women are privileged over other modes of beauty and modesty. American Muslim women are influenced by the Islamic norms of their religious communities but also by the Western ideals of thinness and beauty. This example also illustrates how blog posts which are framed as promoting "health" through fitness, and healthy eating may also be influenced by unhealthy body or gendered standards, and Western sources of these beauty, body and fashion ideals. Thinness is preferred by the Western and Arab fashion industry. Bu thinness can also be an unrealistic and unhealthy ideal. Body diversity is more respected in African communities than in Arab or South Asian communities. But Muslim American and SAMA women in particular are influenced by a combination of western ideals, South Asian norms, and global influences. Where we do see some diversity is both in the Muslim African American community and African cultures. Unfortunately, colonialism's effect on Indian society in particular resulted in fair skin and thin beauty ideals. In the last decade as we see reflected in the blogs, there has been some resistance to unrealistic norms.

HAUTE HIJAB AND DESIGNER MODESTY

Haute Hijab is a Muslim lifestyle blog that came up during conversations with SAMA women. The emphasis on "designer clothing" is what makes Haute Hijab a unique fashion blog, and the key branding on this site is haute couture meets modest attire. The authors explain: "Every idea starts with a problem. Ours is simple: stylish hijabs and hijab friendly clothing is too hard to find. The major retail stores ignore us, and 'cool' brands are too revealing. It turns out we aren't alone in this challenge."

Melanie Elturk and Ahmed Zedan are the site's creators, and since 2010, Haute Hijab has been growing, both as a fashion blog and as an online boutique: "We started Haute Hijab to be that faith-driven modest alternative. . . . By designing all our clothing in-house and engaging with customers directly, we're able to provide high-quality, expertly crafted and uniquely designed hijabs and clothing."

Haute Hijab emphasizes fashion and modest trends for hijabi women. Their readers tend to be upper-class conservative Muslim women who wear hijab. The authors address the challenges to want to wear hijab with their "struggling with hijab" support program, as there is a pull to not wear hijab in a

Muslim minority country especially as political climates change. This classed and religious understanding of modest fashion is emphasized through the content of the articles and the modest products and hijabs the site sells. The references to Quran throughout the website also signal religious identities and a particular interpretation of religious identity.

Food, body, nutrition, and fashion are all recurring themes on Haute Hijab, as well. Haute Hijab has articles on halal food, nutrition during Ramadan, and a hijabi's guide to staying trim. In "A Hijabi's Guide to Eating Healthy and Melanie's Secrets to Staying Trim," Melanie sets up several rules about junk food, eating in moderation, incorporating physical activity, and taking supplements. She cites both the Quran and Hadith as religious reasons as to why Muslim women should eat healthfully and exercise.

The religious and Islamic tone of this site signals religious identity over ethnic or racial identity for its readers as it relies on the Quran and Hadith to establish their religious authority in matters pertaining to health, diet, and fasting all withing an Islamic framework. Lamees Lanham highlights health tips on fasting in "Health Tips to Beat the Fasting Fatigue This Ramadan" which includes food and health tips while fasting by focusing on hydration, suhoor (beginning the fast) and iftar (breaking the fast).

Other food-related posts include a guest post by Saleha Bharde, "9 Quick and Healthy Recipes for The Time-Strapped Woman," which provides recipes including Greek yogurt parfait, hummus wrap and lean burgers for dinner. Haute Hijab overlaps with Hijabican in its themes on modest fashion, food, and the body but it also constructs itself as higher-end lifestyle site.

Haute Hijab does not challenge interpretations of modesty because it is not only focused on wearing hijab but also selling hijab. Haute Hijab is also a commerce site and therefore stays within the framework of neoliberal understandings of "Muslim women," capitalism, and beauty.

MUSLIMGIRL.COM AND THIRD SPACE IDENTITIES

Muslim Girl was created in 2009 as one of the first blogs run by Muslim American women. Though the site initially targeted teenagers and women in their 20s, the readers are now diverse in age, class, ethnicity, and religiosity. The site continues to include important features beyond politics, religion, consumption, and fashion. The posts tend to focus on recurring themes including authenticity and physical appearance, health and food, and lastly politics. Through taking a closer look at how the bloggers look at appearance, food and politics we can get a clearer sense of how Muslim women construct a hybrid identity online.

Muslim Girl is in contrast to the other Muslim sites such as Haute Hijab because it challenges our dominant assumptions about Muslim women. This site has a millennial focus and addresses an expansive range of issues from sexual abuse to career choices and colorism. Muslim Girl has a younger readership, which inspires the authors to continue to evolve their material based on this; additionally, they highlight American Muslim women outside of the dominant images of American Muslim women who wear hijab. Muslim Girl is able to push the boundaries of "Muslim women" by featuring women who wear hijab and others who don't. Darker skinned and larger-sized women as well as Muslim women who don't wear hijab are featured on the site.

Leah Vernon is just one of the African American Muslim bloggers they profile that doesn't fit into the hegemonic standards of thin and light-skinned modest fashion. She is also featured on Muslim Girl both because of her rise as a fashion influencer and because of her progressive politics aligned with Black Lives Matter. Both generation and class shape how Muslim Girl is able to present more progressive understandings of women and Islam as a platform that engages in domestic and global politics. Muslim Girl has addressed Modi's oppression of Muslims in India to the current anti-immigrant rhetoric in the United States. This more political, feminist, and progressive generation becomes more visible in Muslim Girl in an array of voices from the Muslim diaspora reflecting a multiplicity of hybrid identities. However, I am cautious to say that they all share the same progressive politics, as some of the younger feminist political Muslim women are more active in domestic politics in the Trump-era such as participating in anti-racist protests, others are more vocal on global injustices from the treatment of Muslims in Kashmir to China.

Similarly to the other Muslim sites, Muslim Girl includes discussions on consumption, fashion, and modesty. In "How I Use My Sense of Style to Challenge Stereotypes About My Being," Mariam Nouser writes:

> Our patriarchal society tells women, especially racialized women, that we must look like the models we see on the runway. If women are anywhere close to the size that I wear, we are seen as inadequate, and quite frankly, worthless. Now add my Muslim identity to this, and I am truly seen as trash. People think Islam is a monolith, and everyone who identifies as Muslim looks the same. This is an outrageous assumption, and of course there's no truth to it! Yes, some women choose to wear niqabs, hijabs, burqas, skirts, abayas—you name it! But the way we choose to express our faith is only between us and Allah. (April 3, 2019)

The author emphasizes that fashion is about authenticity and not needing to fit in. She also acknowledges both race and patriarchy in her discussions on fashion. Nouser explains that through her fashion choices and clothing, fashion is about authentic self-expression. She acknowledges being simultaneously Muslim and Western, and her stance is a product of Western media and Islamic values.

Under Fit#, the featured articles include stories on cancer, dehydration, trauma, and mental illness. This was also a unique approach to "fit" rather than focusing on just physical fitness, dieting, and body image. Amina Radwan also addresses the body positive movement as it related to Western fashion in "here's-why-im-done-apologizing-for-not-being-a-stick-figure." She writes:

> Women who once loved to possess a voluptuous body type are now struggling to become a woman promoted by Western fashion. . . .Your self-love is worthy and valued . . . Being curvaceous in a society that is increasingly valuing what size zero represents truly teaches you to applaud yourself and accept who you are (Radwan).

Radwan's piece focuses on body acceptance, sizeism, and criticism of unrealistic Western fashion standards. She singles out "Western fashion" and "Western designers" as a source of unrealistic body and fashion norms. Many of the readers of this blog are a product of Western media but also global and Islamic norms. This third space identity is often articulated in particular Islamic and modest ideals that challenge gendered messages embedded in Western media. This interaction results in progressive identity that affirms modest fashion but also embraces western trends.

Even though discussions around recipes, food politics, and health are all categorized under "fit," food's relationship to politics and religion are clearly an important part of the discussion on Muslim Girl. Several of the articles address food and politics, highlighting the hummus wars, Ramadan food, and Palestinian chefs. Through food, Muslim Girl is also able to address both global and domestic politics, such as the Palestinian/Israeli conflict and the Black Lives Matter movement. Zeina Jhaish writes in "7 Palestinian Chefs That Are Doing It for the Culture": "Sadly food is also political, particularly for the Palestinians. This has become abundantly clear as Israel continues its cultural genocide of Palestine through the theft of food culture" (Mar 15, 2019). Palestinian food is one of the more controversial themes on the blog as several of the Muslim lifestyle sites stay away from the Israel and Palestinian conflict. Muslim Girl has also addressed Black Lives Matter as a social justice theme, and its Muslimgirlwoke# section features discussions of social issues and current events including racism, hate crimes, and politics.

While Muslim Girl examines politics in addition to food and fashion, it is also able to address social issues, sexism, and racism through discussions around food, health, clothing, and modesty. Muslim blogs do overlap with Desi blogs, but Desi blogs have broader content, and more diverse readers as the following section explains. SAMA women are often interested in lifestyle blogs that target Desi women (ethnic blogs), as well as those that are aimed at Muslim women (religious blogs).

BROWN GIRL AND DESI BLOGS

The ethnic lifestyle blogs that target Desi or South Asian women have a diverse religious audience often beyond Hindu, Muslim, Sikh, and Christian women. Through looking at Desi lifestyle blogs, we gain a better understanding of gendered, racial, and ethnic identity construction online. Sexuality also intersects with the gendered understandings of these sites. Though heterosexism is the norm in the American Muslim blogs I explored, LGBTQ themes are apparent in the South Asian American blogs. The ethnic online sites aimed at Desi Americans tend to be more expansive in range because they are not constrained by religious ideology. As a result, the diverse South Asian ethnicities on these blogs are often blurred to emphasize a common pan-South Asian culture which includes Bollywood, Hindi language-focused culture, and intersectional challenges encountered by South Asian American females within the American diaspora.

In addition to acknowledging marginalized statuses, these sites emphasize cultural aspects of Desi community identity. Indian culture, film, media, food, and fitness all came up on these blogs and sites. As examples of lifestyle blogs aimed at South Asian American women, I examined Brown Girl, which is aimed at Millennials, tends to have a larger readership of second and third generation women, and has a more inclusive and progressive branding. Brown Girl like Muslim Girl, started as targeting millennials but now has a following of young adults to midcareer professionals.

BROWN GIRLS

"Brown girl" is a slang term that young South Asian American women often use to refer to themselves, so it makes sense as the name of a blog aimed at young South Asian American women. The mission of Brown Girls is stated on their site:

> We empower and engage those who identify as South Asian women living in the diaspora with a hyphenated identity. Through features, interviews, opinion pieces and videos, you'll find a variety of topics covered including trending news, politics, entertainment, beauty, lifestyle, love and relationships, religion and culture.

One of the key overarching themes that makes Brown Girl unique is that it does address current events and politics, in addition to food and fashion. This is a more progressive site, and topics range from racism and politics to religion and sex. The authors continue to push new understandings of ethnic identity and diasporic community without the constraints of conservative ideologies. Brown Girl tries to create an inclusive online community that often challenges the perception of South Asian American women.

Visual media is coded with gendered and racialized representations. Historically, Indian women were portrayed in Bollywood cinema as sexual, thin, and light-skinned. There is an array of representations on Brown Girl that challenges these hegemonic norms, including darker and light skinned, full-figured and thin, and heterosexual and lesbian women. The variety of body types and skin tones representing the multiethnic South Asian global community on Brown Girl is diverse.

As a result of colonialism, Indian media created and reinforced unrealistic, colorist, and racist beauty standards. Colorism can be traced back to the 1940s before India's independence. Colorism was something that was not challenged in the mainstream media in the Indian context until recently. Indian women in particular have been represented as thin and light-skinned in the Bollywood media since the 1950s. The skin-lightening cream Fair and Lovely was introduced in 1975 in the Indian market and spread to Pakistan, Bangladesh, and other South Asian countries (Karnani 2007, 102).

Lewis (2010) writes about the pervasiveness of colorism in her research on American Muslims and fashion: "Colorism, pigment hierarchies are well documented across religious groups in black and Asian cultures; for Muslims, in varied Muslim majority and minority locations and in different diaspora contexts, judgements about skin color may also graft onto discrimination in terms of ethnic and national distinction" (252:8). In particular, Brown Girl addresses colorism within the South Asian American community, and also within India. This is important because Brown Girl not only challenges beauty norms of the Western gaze but also beauty norms from the homeland in South Asia. South Asian women are often valued for their beauty and beauty has traditionally been defined as light-skinned in India and in the American diaspora. As India continues to create Bollywood productions that privilege lighter skinned actresses, Brown Girl chooses to portray images of South Asian women with darker and medium colored skin tones that can help combat this type of prejudice within and outside the communities and to discuss these issues.

Rema Chandan addresses colorism in the post "Bollywood's Unfair and Ugly Obsession with Dark Skin Color" (March 2, 2017). Soon after another piece was posted titled "A Deeper Look into India's Fair Skin Obsessed Beauty Standards" which critiques the ads of Fair and Lovely in India (May

26, 2017). In 2018, Brown Girl posted a piece titled "Your Natural Skin Is Beautiful: Conquering Colorism in the South Asian Community" (March 31, 2018). Colorism not only affects South Asian women's self-esteem or confidence during adolescence, but colorism also plays a role in arranging marriages.

In addition to colorism, a second important type of prejudice that Brown Girl addresses is sizeism, which aligns the site with the body positive movements. Brown Girl highlights varying types of bodies but also addresses body positive themes. In 2014, the blog highlighted the *Mindy Project* as an example of an Indian American actress with a darker skin and a "normal" body (not thin). Bhutani explains that Mindy Kaling is more representative of what South Asian American women really look like, both in terms of her size and skin color.:

> Here is a woman starring on her own show who looks like us! (For us brown girls both in body shape and skin color!) And she is capable of dressing nicely and having romantic encounters with men! Ah! All this time Hollywood and Bollywood has told us that we must look like some kind of bombshell if we want to attract attractive men. Mindy proves this wrong. Off-screen, Mindy is just as fierce. The girl wears whatever she wants and looks good. (Bhutani August 15, 2014).

In 2016, the blog promoted Kripa Joshi's "Miss Moti" which translates to "Miss Fat." "Miss Moti" is another example of a media icon who is also not thin. Chhaye Nene wrote in 2016:

> The artist is experiencing a wide range of success following the publishing of her comics, which readers say allow them to promote a positive body image. Moti means plump or large in Hindi. However, the way Joshi wants readers to [say] it is by pronouncing the T slightly differently so that it could mean a pearl, also spelt as moti in Hindi.

A closer analysis of this character can be interpreted as seeing a larger-sized woman as a jewel and valued as a treasured object of high value (Nene, August 19, 2016). In 2017, Sejal Sehimi examined Bollywood's fat-shaming culture. In this piece, the author highlighted the problems with assuming that a plus-size character is assumed to be the comic relief. Sehmi writes:

> As far back as my childhood memories serve me, the on-screen arrival of a "plus-size" female actor in a Bollywood film often prompted the audience to assume "ah, that must be the heroine's fat funny friend!" . . . However, this smart lady used her stint on the dance reality show, "Nach Baliye," to finally call out on society's fat-shaming culture.

Sehmi's piece expands on how the roles assigned to actresses in Bollywood reinforce sizeism and fat shaming culture, but in 2017, Bharti Singh used her fame to actually challenge Bollywood's fat shaming culture.

In addition to colorism and sizeism, Brown Girl also examines sexuality and homophobia. The topic of sexuality is often absent in blogs and lifestyle media sites created by Muslim women because these blogs tend to reinforce heterosexism and adhere to conservative Islamic norms, but blogs and sites created by non-Muslim South Asian women tend to be more inclusive when it comes to sexuality, ethnicity, race, and religion. There are some ideological differences in how American Muslims, even in the diaspora, approach homosexuality, but there has traditionally been a conservative interpretation of homosexuality by dominant Islamic organizations globally and in North America. More recently scholars have debated how to address or even incorporate the LGBTQ community into the North American Muslim community, and there is now an active LGBTQ friendly mosque in Toronto and a small presence is growing in the United States. These changes are significant, but homophobia is still present in much of the Muslim diaspora (Habib 2016).

When blogs like Brown Girl address LGBTQ issues, it is a result of second and third generation immigrants' resistance to hegemonic and conservative norms (Ocampo 2016). Desi lesbians have a higher likelihood of coming out in the American diaspora if they have support (Magpantay 2016). Brown Girl *has* addressed LGBTQ issues in several important features. In 2018, the site posted: "How to Find the One as a Brown LGBTQ Girl" by Varsha Mathur. Mathur writes about the struggles of being a Desi American queer woman. In 2018, the blog added a feature called "Queering Desi." One of the pieces was titled "#NotMyBinary: Deconstructing the Gender Binary with Our Friendly Neighborhood Brown LGBTQ Superheroes." Brown Girl also examined changing advertising in India in regard to LGBTQ representation when in 2015, the blog highlighted "India's First Lesbian Ad Is a Big Step toward Social Change in a Conservative Country"; this adds an important transnational lens from the younger diaspora.

In addition to challenging norms around sexuality, colorism, and body size, Brown Girl also offers diverse models of womanhood and gender roles including career/professional women working outside the home and stay at home mothers. The Indian woman as a traditional homemaker is a common gendered stereotype that is reinforced in Indian society through families, religion, and media, much like it is reinforced throughout the Western diaspora. Desi women are expected to be educated and professionally successful, but also have a partner, children, and maintain a household. These women are often seen as model minority success stories while simultaneously being socialized into gendered and patriarchal understandings of womanhood.

Brown Girl addresses many of these contradictions and challenges. There are often posts on balancing motherhood with work, such as "Meet Rita Kakati Shah: The Wonder Woman Helping Other Mothers Transition Back to the Workforce," by Bushra Rahman, and "Dear New Mom: Don't Forget to Love Yourself, Too," by Anisha Pandya Patel. This site also highlights successful professional women with children in features on successful female entrepreneurs such as "Shilpa Shah of Cuyana Gives Meaning to 'Seeking Fulfillment over Balance' on the Heels of Her First New York City Brick and Mortar." An analysis of the blogs aimed at Desi women is reveals how they challenge stereotypes of Asian women, increase representation in social media, and present alternative understandings of Desi norms for women. Instagram is another important mode of analysis for examining Desi and Muslim women.

MODEST FASHION ON INSTAGRAM

Instagram is an important site for sociological research because of its representation of minority women, including Muslim women who adhere to modesty norms but also disrupt the "Muslim fashion" narrative of thin, light skinned hijabi women (Lewis 2015). Fashion, consumption, and identity formation are seen throughout Instagram accounts, while political imagery is woven into the accounts more subtly than in the blogs. Images allow for symbolic messages in a way that textual analysis does not.

Since the creation of Instagram, we've seen the increasing visibility of diverse women of varying body size, color, and background in social media. Nabeela Noor, who is a plus-sized South Asian Muslim influencer does not wear hijab. Leah Vernon does wear hijab, and she is African American and also plus sized. On Instagram, we see an array of representations of modest fashion and Muslim influencers of diverse ethnicities, skin colors, and sizes.

Looking at female Muslim Instagrammers reveals challenges of what it means to be a Muslim woman on social media. Though Instagram was primarily a photo sharing platform, in addition to reading the visual rhetoric images, a closer analysis of likes, comments, and discussions reveals significant themes and highlights how visual representation of self is related to the themes of class, ethnicity, religion, and gendered performance. I argue that Instagram selfies are an important medium for understanding the intersectional performance of self not solely based on visual representations. The ways that these intersectional identities are formed online are in constant negotiation because of the conversation followers have with the microcelebrity via likes and comments.

In many ways, what we see on Instagram can be compared to the diversity found in Muslim Girl or Brown Girl. Modest Instagram influencers and hijabi microcelebrities reinforce Western notions of beauty through gendered ideals but often use their agency to challenge dominant representations of the body. On Instagram, we see the hashtags #ModestMuslim and #MuslimFashion pull up an array of images including Muslim women in hijab to Arab, South Asian, and African American women dressed modestly but not wearing hijab, to Muslim women that are plus sized.

Among the hijabi and Muslim microcelebrities, luxury accessories such as designer shoes, bags, and sunglasses in particular are used to reproduce social status hierarchies. Alice Marwick (2015) argues that Instafame reinforces inequality through luxury goods and social capital via increased followers. Peterson (2017) adds that Instagram is a place where Muslim women negotiate their "authentic" Muslim identities through consumption. Several of the Instagram stars that I examine represent their religious identities through visual images like mosques, scarves, or prayer mats, whether or not they wear hijab. They also negotiate their gender identities through fashion, clothing, accessories, and makeup; they signal their religious identities through references to religious holidays, scripture, or mosques; and their class status is coded through food and vacation.

Muslims also engage in political commentary and body politics. These communities are in conversation with other influencers, their commenters, and the changing national and global political climates, which often reflect a narrative of anxiety. Following 9/11, and then more recently under the Trump presidency, Muslim influencers are able to exert some agency in how they portray their consumption patterns but also in terms of how they engage with conversations on politics and religion. The online representations of Muslim women on Instagram often mediate the need to represent their bicultural identities but also politicize their Muslim or ethnic identities, especially as cosmopolitan consumers.

The Instagram accounts I examine belong to Muslim influencers who all have endorsements from well-known brands, from Converse to Bloomingdales, but they have also curated a following amongst other Muslim women. Marwick (2015) defines microcelebrity, as those social media users who create profiles, engage with followers, and use their personal information to increase their online status. Influencers are those social media personalities who are being compensated by corporations, usually through paid advertising or product endorsements (Abidin 2015). By growing their online following, Hijabi Instagrammers are also increasing their social capital through growing their online networks.

HIJABI MUSLIM MICROCELEBRITIES: MARIA ALIA, FATIMA ALI, AND SUMMER ALBARCHA

Maria Alia, Fatima Ali, and Summer Albarcha are three of the Instagram microcelebrities I studied closely because they all had a following of more than one hundred thousand accounts. In many ways, they represent the future of cosmopolitan consumption among Western middle-class Muslim women.

Maria Alia Al-Sadek is a 27-year-old Palestinian American based in New York City. She's had an Instagram account since 2012. As of October 2019, she had over 429,000 followers. Her average selfie has 12,000 likes and one hundred comments. She began wearing hijab at age 14. Maria Alia's account is an interesting fashion account shaped by Muslim, Palestinian, American, and upper middle-class identities. Maria Alia signals all of these multiple identities through her images and textual captions. Though she wears hijab, she maintains a high fashion wardrobe. She has hundreds of images where she is wearing hijab along with luxury accessories. While some Muslim women believe that modesty is about wearing loose clothing and covering the hair, some women in my interviews also spoke about modesty as being more about maintaining simple (modest) as opposed to presumptuous displays of wealth or beauty (see chapter 2 interviews). Maria Alia told Bloomberg, "Everyone has their own interpretation of modesty. . . . But this idea that it's just a very plain, no adornment, humble way of dressing—that was some other person's definition" (bloomberguint.com). A closer examination of modest fashion through Muslim microcelebrities reveals the multiple ways that faith and fashion are represented.

In addition to gender, religion and class shape the accounts of Muslim microcelebrities such as Maria Alia through a mix of fashion trends, modest clothing, and politics. Maria Alia embodies global cosmopolitan consumption in the construction of her online profile via Instagram through luxury brands, modesty, and political awareness. Her accessories signal her upper-class status, and her clothing choices reflect conservative modesty norms. Class is also reflected in her luxury accessories, travel and food. She does wear makeup, which you can see in her close-up selfies. She wears jewelry, including large earrings and the turban style hijab. In her pictures, she usually wears longs skirts or long pants. Her gender and class are reflected in her accessories and wardrobe. In a November 9, 2019 post, she wears oversize gold hoop earrings, manicured gold nails and bold gold eyeshadow. The post has over 6,000 likes and over seventy comments. As you look closer at the image, you can see she has tagged all the brand names she is wearing, which shows she is successful in branding, marketing, and self-promotion.

Her back and forth with readers helps her develop a global online community of female Muslim followers. These online communities may be fleeting but they are places that Western Muslim women come together to share, discuss, and negotiate modesty and fashion. Maria Alia signals gender and femininity through her fashion choices and represents her faith through images of modesty, references to mosques, Ramadan, and scripture. She reveals her class through references to food and international travel. She discusses modesty directly in her turban tutorial. She wears the turban style of hijab, which reveals her ears and neck like the hoodjabi, and as a result she is able to wear certain accessories and jewelry (chapter 2). On January 22, 2020, she posted a preview of her Nike campaign in hijab.

Unlike some other modest Instagrammers, Maria Alia wears bold makeup. For example, on November 13, 2017, she wears full @lorealmakeup look and is wearing a red bold lipstick. This image has over 10,000 likes and over one hundred comments. Maria demonstrates how to appear modest but fashion-forward and Western; her style is an inspiration to her followers. She often wears designer accessories like Chanel sandals, a Prada tote, and a Carolina Herrera bag. On November 12, 2019, she featured an image of a Louis Vuitton designer bag with LVs. She also signals her class status through images from international travel. She has Instagram posts from faraway places like Greece and France. On March 19, 2016, she posted breakfast in Paris.

Maria Alia's posts also address global politics. She refers to Palestine in her pictures at the Lebanese border in several 2019 Instagram posts. On July 21, 2019, she posted from the Lebanon border and the caption reads, "Watch my 'home.' Highlight for the full journey. No words for how returning to my family's home in Palestine felt. Heart is full and heavy." Two days earlier, her Instagram post was the Palestinian flag with a caption that read: "My dad grew up in a Palestinian refugee camp in Lebanon—it's really a full circle moment to be in the very land that my ancestors called home but were never able to return home to. I'm so blessed and grateful for this trip." This post received 166 comments and 16,471 likes.

Maria Alia is a Muslim microcelebrity who is simultaneously religious, fashion conscious and political. She constructs how her faith and fashion, in addition to her politics, shape her consumption practices as a cosmopolitan Muslim woman. In contrast, the bloggers of Haute Hijab and Hijabican are focused on religion and fashion and tend to stay away from politics.

Secondly, I turn to the Muslim influencer Fatima Abdullah also known as Fatima Ali whose account is called All Things Fatima. Fatima Ali is a hijabi influencer also based in New York City. Her tag line is "Just a modest fashion gal in NYC." Her account was created in 2016, and as of November 2019, she had over 118,000 followers. In the "about" portion of her Instagram account, she writes "Just a mix between fashion, faith, and feminism." Fatima is a Muslim Palestinian American, and her posts focus on fashion, food, beauty, and politics.

On April 7, 2017, Fatima Abdullah was quoted in the BBC article, "This is what it's like to wear a hijab and live in Donald Trump's America, saying women she knows, can't take the staring anymore and that's why they've decided to abandon the hijab. . . . There's a lack of tolerance for who we are and how we dress. I feel like it's made hate more tolerable now in our society." Fatima says her ambition is to help others feel comfortable wearing a hijab (BBC, April 7, 2017). This quote implies that at least some Muslim women who don't wear hijab really want to but since Trump became president, hesitate because of the increased intolerance and threat of being stared at or intimidated. Fatima's comments suggest she interprets modesty as wearing hijab but also points out the reality faced by hijab-wearers in the Trump era. Her reference to "hate more tolerable" also is a reference to the increase in xenophobia and Islamaphobia in particular. Since 2016, there has been a documented increase in hate crimes in the United States against Muslims, Jews, and racial minorities.

Fatima wears her hijab both in the traditional style covering her neck, and also in the non-traditional turban style. Looking at her past Instagram posts, we see the themes of fashion and gender through her use of clothing, jewelry, and makeup. Her religious identity is seen through her signaling of religious holidays such as Eid. In addition her class status is apparent through her luxury accessories and food images. A closer look at her images and posts reveal how she presents her political beliefs along with her sense of fashion and faith. She often wears her political accessories. For example, in 2019, she is wearing a sweater cardigan with jeans and a necklace with a small pendant of Palestine. The post says, "Always keeping Palestine on my mind and close to my heart, thanks to $paliroots necklaces" (November 12, 2019).

In 2018, she posted has an Instagram image that reads, "#GazaBleeds" against a black background. This post received over 2,000 likes and twenty comments (May 26, 2018). The caption reads, "Currently raising money through @unrwa to feed families in need throughout Gaza. As many of you may know Gaza is labeled by the UN as the world's largest open-air prison, nothing and no one is allowed in or out and so the people of Gaza are in dire need of the many basic necessities that we take for granted such as food. So I would be so grateful to anyone that makes a contribution (no matter how big or small) to this cause." She received 861 likes but only two comments.

Her posts on food signal her class status; on November 2, 2017, she posted an image from Manhattan's Laduree bakery. Laduree is a Paris-based bakery that opened franchises in New York City in the last decade and is an example of affluent culinary consumption. Laduree only has locations in large and wealthy cities like Manhattan, London, and Paris, and tends to serve affluent "foodies." Similar to the women interviewed in chapter 1, Muslim Instagrammers food choices are shaped by middle class status.

Her posts around her Muslim identity tend to focus on religious holidays such as Eid and Ramadan. On, May 31, 2019, she posted a picture of herself from the back wearing a brown hijab with sunglasses and a green long-sleeved dress. The caption reads, "I still can't believe we are in the last few days of Ramadan. These are the most powerful days of the year. . . . I've partnered this Ramadan with @humancaresyri, to raise funds for food packages to be distributed to Syrian families affected by the war there." This comment is typical of how religious identity and fashion often intersect with political identities in her posts. In 2019, she posted her own image in a black hijab and a polka dot long-sleeved blouse. The caption reads, "I know I'm super late in posting but Happy Eid to all of you that celebrated. Hope your day's [*sic*] were full of love and laughter and I pray all our fasting in this past month was accepted. Much love [*sic*]" (June 26, 2019). She received 2,500 likes and forty-nine comments.

In 2017 she posted a video clip from BBC player "NY Hijabis." Her caption reads, "I'm both grateful and excited to announce the international release of the @bbcradio1 documentary *NYHijabis!* The documentary embodies the diversity of Muslim women and celebrates their resilience to be unapologetically themselves in a Post-Trump America. I'm humbled to have been part of such a raw piece with some amazing influencers" (April 7, 2017).

Her posts also interject her stance on national politics. In 2017, she posted an image of the *New York Times* and her caption reads: "constantly reading about the tragedy @Charlottesville, still waiting to read about our government taking proper action against it" (August 21, 2017). She received 998 likes and four comments.

Fatima Ali and Maria Alia are similar in how they create their Instagram profiles through signaling their religious identities, politics, and class status. However, as a hijab or modest microcelebrity, Fatima Ali has more mentions of national politics whereas Maria Alia has more references to global politics. Both are signaling their class status through luxury accessories, high fashion, and travel.

The third account that I turn to is that of one of the original "hispster hijabis," Summer Albarcha. She opened her Instagram account in 2012 as hipsterhijabis where she now has over five hundred thousand followers. Her first post on August 2, 2012, was an image of a note that said, "Welcome to hipsterhijabis! We hope to inspire you with our modest, yet fashionable look. Don't worry. . . . Pictures will be coming soon." Albarcha, a 22-year-old Instagram influencer was born and raised in the United States, though her parents are from Syria. Her average selfie has four thousand likes, and she does respond to followers.

Unlike Maria Ali, Summer Albarcha wears the hijab in the traditional way, which means her hijab covers her hair and earrings. She does wear long necklaces on occasion, but her neck and ears are always covered along with her hair. Her tagline is "Digital Creator" and "I Love Layering." She is based in New York City and has a YouTube channel as well. On her website's page, titled "Meet Summer Albarcha, Creative Director," her bio is as follows:

> Summer Albarcha began in 2012 as Hipster Hijabis, a modest fashion blog for teenagers in the St. Louis area. At the age of eighteen, she was invited to Dubai to speak at Fashion Forward to address the lack of modest fashion trends in the United States. Summer soon learned her blogging could make a difference and decided to develop her profile and her love of fashion throughout her college career as Summer Albarcha.

Summer's Instagram account signaled religion, class, gender, and politics. Most visibly, Summer's Instagram account is marked by her religious identity through her adherence to wearing hijab and observance of Muslim holidays including Eid and Ramadan. On August 18, 2012, she posted an image of herself from the neck down, showing the bottom of her hijab with a sweater, long skirt, and bag and the caption reads, "Possible inspiration for your Eid outfit." On July 21, 2004, she posted a picture in an abaya (long over-coat often worn for prayers) and hijab and the caption reads, "Accessorizing my abaya with these #posttareeweeh late night snacks (since my daytime snacking is being put on hold)" She received 423 likes (July 21, 2004). Post-taraweehah late night snacks refers to midnight snacking after the additional Islamic prayers that are only performed in Ramadan (the thirty days of fasting). The posting of holiday celebrations such as Eid is a common theme in all the Muslim Instagram accounts here.

INSTAGRAMMER SHEHZEEN: THE DESI WONDER WOMAN

In addition to looking at hijabi Instagram influencers, I looked at the account of a modest microcelebrity who calls herself the "Desi Wonder Woman." Shehzeen is a Pakistani Australian immigrant based in Sydney, Australia. She has over 54,000 followers and is a full-time lifestyle blogger and Instagram microcelebrity with both Muslim and Desi followers. She posts on fashion, food, and sometimes her Muslim and Pakistani Australian identity. Her tag line is "Fulltime blogger, part-time napper, give me your chai." Through her clothes, accessories, and food, we learn about her ethnic and middle-class identity. Her posts on being Muslim are largely related to celebrating holidays such as Ramadan and Eid. She does signal her ethnic, and class identity as being Pakistani-Australian, but she seldom posts on politics. Through her posts on food, she does acknowledge the process of food production and sustainability.

On July 15, 2019, Shehzeen posted a picture of three Pakistani dishes, and shared her ethics around food consumption:

> Making an average day kinda fancy with a grand spread of three whole dishes for a regular weeknight dinner. Leftover aloo, leftover baingnan, and leftover daal."But aging is an experience that I think helps you find for respect for food (and maybe just about everything) in a very macroscopic manner. Not just where you become more aware of how so many people don't have access to even one meal a day. But also in terms of the whole agricultural supply chain—from the farmers that work for days on end, the crops that take months to grow. The quiet journey from the farm to the trader, the distributor, the retailer, to our markets, to our homes and then finally to our tables. One bite of your meal today is the product of months of intensive labor. We value things like gems and stones because they're priced higher so who would consider tossing them away. But food, because cheap, ends up in our waste more times than we can remember. Even when we dispose of it ethically, there's a connect than gets lost between the value of our money and the respect for how we earned that meal.

The meal she refers to consists of leftovers of potato curry, spicy eggplant, and lentil stew that she cooked the day before when she is making this post and is referencing reheated dishes. Shehzeen references an ethical consciousness about food production and even recycling as she comments "even when we dispose of it ethically." In this post, she expresses some awareness of her class privilege when she writes, "more aware of how so many people don't have access to even one meal a day" and also references farm worker's labor when she writes: "But also in terms of the whole agricultural supply chain—from the farmers that work for days on end."

Shehzeen's posts on food and clothing reveal her biccultural and religious identities. She posts in Western outfits such as dresses, jeans, or pants, but on occasion around Eid or religious celebrations, she has posted images of herself in a salwar kameez. In 2018, she posted in a salwar kameez wearing a long flowy dupatta. The caption reads, "I'm dying to wear shalwar kameez/desi clothes. Still cold here so gots to wait a couple months before it can happen. Old picture from the old timez. #pakistansindabaad (October 8, 2018). The variety of images of clothing evidence her bicultural and hybrid identity. On March 28, 2017, she posted an outfit with a plain white kurta, jeans, and a colorful dupatta, with the caption, "Today's action: Dupatta from

Bahawalpur, jeans from gap. Bag from @sheinofficial, Khuassas from @chaptr13."

Shehzeen's posts also reveal her religious identity through travel. On August 21, 2008, she posted pictures of a light fixture from her trip to haj. Her text reads:

> I never realized the significance of this time until my own journey last August. Haj Mubarak to those who were able to do it this year. Hope it brings harmony and order to your lives for the days to come and you're able to live the promise beyond this short, physical journey. The easy part is over, staying committed to your Haj is much tougher than the steps you take on food. I hope we can all keep it breathing for as long as we are here. Wish you your trips back home, safe and in peace. Haj Mubarak, hajis. #haj2018 #hajj (August 21, 2018).

She received 1,000 likes and fourteen comments. The haj trip is the pilgrimage to Mecca and is considered one of the five pillars of Islam. Observant Muslims tend to go on this trip at least once in their lifetime, if they can afford it.

Analyzing Instagram influencers in addition to looking at lifestyle blogs, helps paint a more complete picture of how Muslim women construct their identities online. Desi Muslim Instagrammers, along with modest influencers, paint an ever evolving and sophisticated picture of Muslim women. Hybrid identities in Instagram indicate agency and autonomy but also address the constraints of capitalism, religion, and patriarchy. The nuanced differences highlight how intersectional representations often vary. In particular, Instagram helps highlight the class component of identity for Muslim microcelebrities and modest influencers through images of travel, food, clothing and luxury accessories. Hegemonic femininity, "desi bling," and religious symbols all play an important role in these online negotiations, revealing that hijabi influencers and modest microcelebrities are not a monolithic group. African American Muslim women like Leah Vernon and plus-size microcelebrities like Nabeela Noor in particular further complicate this narrative. Queer and bi-microcelebrities like Umber Ghauri who have darker skin and don't adhere to modesty norms also present challenges to hegemonic understandings of Muslim fashion.

CONCLUSION

Social media has multiple functions for SAMA women including creating an online community, reinforcing and challenging religious, gendered, or cultural norms around food and dress, and creating sites of resistance and alternative consumption options. Sites like Hijabican and Haute Hijab often attempt to discourage women from buying clothing or scarves from multinational corporations, encouraging them to support Muslim-owned businesses instead. Blogs aimed at Desi or South Asian American women are often a place where a racialized and gendered minority can come together as an online community. They can discuss politics, racism, sexism, homophobia, changes in American society, and issues of representation.

In addition to blogs, Instagram plays an increasing role in how SAMA women choose to represent themselves. Religion, class, gender, and sometimes politics play a role in the way modest Instagrammers in particular construct their online identities. These images often paint a contradictory image of Muslim women as they are modest and religious, but also active consumers and agents in a global capitalist marketplace. Faith and fashion will continue to play a role online, but political content may increase as both the national and global climates may shift how American Muslim women and immigrants are perceived in the American landscape.

Conclusion

Khaleda heads to Whole Foods to pick up some organic cilantro to cook with the chicken that's marinating in garam masala and yogurt at home. She's wearing a Michael Kors tunic and a leopard-print, black and brown scarf as her hijab. In between picking out the cilantro and heading to the register, she returns an email from her daughter and replies, "Yes, order me one of those dresses linked to Modenesia's website —I think Saba recommended that from her last trip."

Khaleda's consumption practices, like those of other SAMA women, are coded with her class, her religion, and her gender. What she eats and wears, where and how she shops, and which social media she uses and how she uses it are all shaped by both her individual identity and the collective identities of the groups to which she belongs. Her choices to shop at Whole Foods and to wear clothing by the famous designer Michael Kors are common practices among upper-middle class Americans. Adding the hijab to her outfit allows her to blend in her religious identity, which requires modest dress. She chooses the leopard print to blend her American fashion sense with her ethnic wardrobe. The cilantro and other foods she purchases help her connect to her ethnic identity, which she also embraces (along with her religion) by choosing online modest clothing vendors popular among SAMA community members, like her friend Saba.

Khaleda's practices are not unique to her experience—many SAMA immigrant women shop at luxury or chain grocery stores, purchase halal meat, and order modest clothing online. However, SAMA women negotiate these different identities in diverse ways. For instance, they understand and observe halal and modesty rules in a whole spectrum of ways. Among the SAMA women in this study, my findings revealed a wide range of consumption choices as well as a wide range of the ideologies, identities, and lived experiences that influence them.

Though race, class, gender, and religion shape the consumption patterns of SAMA women, the political climate also frames how these factors play out. For example, after 9/11 some halal restaurants saw a loss in business, and some of my subjects decided to stop wearing hijab. I began this project in 2015, the year before Donald Trump was elected president of the United States. Many SAMA women protested the Trump administration from the beginning. Signs of resistance among Muslim women famously included the iconic image of the American flag worn as hijab in Shepard Fairey's inaugural protest poster,[1] and also through American women creating and wearing "pussy hats." Unfortunately, the marginalization of Asian immigrants, Muslims, and women continued to increase under Trump's presidency. The Muslim ban, the quota on refugees, the increase in Islamophobia, and the increase in racial profiling have all shaped the lives of SAMA women. Under Trump, resistance became a strong theme in the American Muslim and immigrant narratives. Though resisting was first communicated on social media, the Muslim community continued resisting by maintaining traditional identities in their religious congregations and ethnic communities.

Though existing stigmatization of Muslims, immigrants of color, and people of color more generally has grown, SAMA women have continued to maintain modesty norms. In fact, "Muslim fashion" has taken off in the last decade. The prevalence of Instagram and lifestyle blogs devoted to Muslim fashion has grown while fashion magazines, advertisement campaigns, clothing stores, and even museums have also paid tribute to modest fashion. The exhibit "Contemporary Muslim Fashions" opened at the Cooper Hewitt Smithsonian Design Museum in Manhattan in February 2020.[2] Nike embraces hijabi sportswear, and high-end fashion shows, including the 2016 New York Fashion Week, feature modest fashion. Halal food has a national and global presence (Mejova, Benkhedda, and Khairani 2007) and halal foodies have an Instagram visibility. SAMA women continue to embrace their hybrid identities, often through fashion and food. Many of these negotiations take place in online spaces and thus the internet continues to foster community for marginalized voices.

Consumption of food, dress, and social media provide important arenas for minority communities, especially those that have limited representation in the American society and mainstream media, to create their own collective ethnic, religious, and gendered identities. Through social media in particular, we can more closely see how these hybrid identities also shape SAMA women's omnivorous and cosmopolitan consumption patterns. They are buying brands popular in the general American public; they are "doing gender" and "doing difference" through consumption (West and Zimmerman 1987; West and Fenstermaker 1997).

FOOD CONSUMPTION

Using food to maintain ethnic identity has been an American way of preserving collective identities for all immigrants from Italian to Chinese and Mexican immigrants, but using food to maintain ethnic, religious, classed, gender and political identity is enhanced for SAMA immigrants. Middle-class food trends are often reflected in the food practices of South Asian immigrants. In addition to maintaining ethnic food, many in this group also strive to eat healthy, organic, and sometimes halal or local. How they prioritize each of these factors is contingent on their cultural, political, religious, and classed identities.

This research confirms that SAMA women are often the ones who are still "feeding the family," and the food traditions that are passed on to the next generation are done so by the women in the family (DeVault 1991). Through food, we preserve cultural tradition and religious practices, understand gender norms, and observe how class shapes consumption options. Patriarchy and culture also shape how collective identity is formed and maintained. Women have performed the invisible added labor of maintaining and passing ethnic identity on through food and clothing in SAMA families.

Our food choices say something about who we are or who we want to be perceived as. For example, if we choose to buy local or fair trade, we may be trying to align our consumption practices with our values. Ethical consumption encompasses many aspects of food but also clothing, and social media. Examining foodways for SAMA women helps us understand how they negotiate between their middle-class American statuses, their ethnic identities, and their religious values. Negotiating between these is just one way that SAMA women do the work of fitting in to all of their various communities.

CLOTHING CONSUMPTION

Though Americans outside of Muslim communities may imagine that SAMA women are highly restricted in dress, Muslim consumers in this study ultimately revealed is that there is no monolithic way to be a Muslim woman or to be "Desi." Garment choices and styles give SAMA women autonomy in creating their hybrid wardrobes. These decisions are shaped by economic, cultural, and social capital. Both geographical and financial access to garments continues to shape wardrobes, though online shopping has improved access to modest and ethnic options.

Shopping is often a way for SAMA women to socialize. Though SAMA women do shop online, many still go to brick-and-mortar stores. Shopping in physical stores allows women to better assess the fit, modesty, and quality of the garments. But more importantly, going to brick and mortar stores has a social component and can be a female-bonding experience. Through shopping together, women seek validation and exchange advice. Many women in my study spoke about shopping with a friend, sister, or mother, which shows that shopping remains a viable social activity for SAMA women even in the Internet era. For example, Diba talked about shopping with her mother. Azka spoke about shopping with her friends. Junnah spoke about how she texts her mother images of salwar kameezes as a form of social interaction and staying in touch. These findings suggest that shopping is often a way of doing gender for SAMA women (West and Zimmerman 1987).

Women also preserve ethnic traditions through clothing. Collective ethnic identities for heteronormative SAMA women are often maintained through gendered identities. Heterosexual, married SAMA women also spoke about their own mothers and mothers-in-law shopping for salwar kameezes and other types of ethnic clothing for them. Hijabs were brought back from Michigan, and salwar kameezes were brought back from Pakistan by female relatives. They creatively put together wardrobes they understand as on trend but also modest. These wardrobes are a negotiation of faith and fashion, which reflect SAMA women's hybrid identities that result from a combination of local, global, and religious factors.

THIRD SPACE IDENTITIES AND MULTIPLE WARDROBES

Though SAMA women's ethnic South Asian wardrobes are shaped by global trends originating in India or Pakistan, their modest wardrobes are much more nuanced. For those who wear hijab, the norms shaping hijab and hair coverings come from the Middle East and Africa, depending on which style of hijab is being practiced; traditional forms of hijab that cover the neck and ears originate in the Middle East, while the hair coverings that leave the neck and ears unadorned are referred to as the "turban" style. Zeenat spoke about the influence from the American Muslim community including trends like the hoodjabi, which is often traced to Chicago (Khabeer 2016).

Where earlier studies of modest fashion have focused solely on Muslim women who covered their hair, this study has expanded that research to assert that modest Muslim women construct their wardrobes in an array of forms. This research also emphasizes that the diversity of practices of modesty among SAMA women is shaped by cultural norms, religious norms, and classed norms, all patterns which are well documented in ever-changing social media. In fact, social media is often where we can see these negotiations between faith, fashion, global, and local trends play out, as we saw in chapter 3. To complicate matters further, Muslim fashion does include women who do not cover their hair, as we see in the Instagram accounts of Shehzeen or Nabeela Noor and on the blog Muslim Girl.

Hijab as a choice in the Western diaspora has been established by many scholars, and the negotiating of a gendered and ethnic wardrobe shaped by culture and religion, has been discussed as a particular way of "doing gender" (Zimmerman and West 1987). Outsiders looking in might interpret extravagant jewelry, bright makeup, and ornate saris or salwar kameezes as hyper-feminine, but these wardrobes are coded in quite nuanced and intersectional ways by immigrant/ethnic and religious identities. How one wears their hijab, the type of salwar kameez chosen, and the choice to wear jewelry or makeup all have meaning.

For insiders, fashion and clothing are layered with symbols; though outsiders may see cultural wardrobes as monolithic, they are sophisticated and layered in how they signal religious, cultural, and classed identities. Wearing a hand-made salwar kameez with wide leg salwars from Lahore's 2018 spring line is coded with as much meaning or status as dark-wash skinny jeans from 2014. SAMA women in this study noted the difference in status associated with purchasing ready-made salwar kameezes from local Chicago boutiques on Devon Avenue versus having custom salwar kameezes made in Pakistan. Other women spoke about purchasing designer handbags and sunglasses but buying their tunics and jeans at the Loft and H&M. Modest influencers like Shehzeen exemplify both hybrid and omnivorous consumption on Instagram.

SOCIAL MEDIA

Social media is really at the center of much that happens for contemporary SAMA women around food, clothing, and all other consumption. Social media is also the conduit for sharing and finding food inspiration and influence. Social media affords SAMA women access to alternative shopping sites, collective identity, and social bonding through online shopping. Instagram often links to other platforms like blogs and tweets, and within images there are corporate tags that direct viewers to sites where they can purchase clothing.

In examining a small slice of blogs and Instagram accounts, the study demonstrates how dynamic and layered these spaces are. In addition to food, travel, and wardrobes, social media also encompasses the consumption and negotiation of religion and politics. Instagram can be used to examine and reveal shifting political and religious identities by documenting visual codes that signal messages to insiders that outsiders often miss. As largely a visual online platform, Instagram has a unique function in allowing marginalized groups to connect in overt and subtle ways through coded images and visual language.

Instagram posts about food and fashion reveal class, but also political and religious perspectives. For example, a picture of a croissant from Laduree reveals cultural capital and status because Laduree is a French bakery chain that specializes in macarons and desserts.. An image of leftover curries is used to talk about food waste and sustainability. An image of a SAMA woman not wearing hijab but wearing an Allah charm necklace, tunic, and leggings indicates a level of modesty and piousness. On Instagram, we can literally watch negotiations between different perspectives on modesty take place as influencers or modest micro-celebrities "role model" how to be both pious and fashionable.

Recent research has looked closely at how social media is used to study religion, fashion, and economics (Lewis 2013). But even within the study of faith and fashion, the array of interpretations of how modest fashion materializes in social media has been understudied to overemphasize hijab. This book broadens that scope and affirms that there are a variety of ways that Muslim women display modesty in person, as discussed in chapter 2, and also online, as mentioned in chapter 3. Modest fashion includes hijab and veiled women but also includes women who choose not to wear the hijab.

The politics of modesty often intersect with hybrid identities in the recent political climate. Trump-era misogyny, anti-immigrant rhetoric, and racism framed how SAMA women negotiated these modest options. SAMA women debate modesty norms on Muslim blogs like Haute Hijab and in conversation with modest Instagrammers like Summer Albarcha. Instagram shows us the diverse, complicated, and often contradictory ways that modest fashion is practiced. Among both those who wear the hijab and those who do not, there is a spectrum of belief about how acceptable different styles of hijab are, the role of earrings, or what uses and types of makeup are widely accepted. Modest fashion as seen on Instagram also reinforces class hierarchies through the consumption of makeup and luxury accessories.

In addition to accessories, food and travel also play a role in how SAMA women present themselves online. Food plays a frequent role in selfies, whether they show eating Laduree macarons or a Big Mac from McDonalds. Food is often an important prop that symbolizes status or body image, but food can also be symbolic of faraway destinations and travel. Food is almost always intertwined with class. Social media is a place where faith, food, and fashion are negotiated by SAMA women online. These negotiations on Instagram, as well as fashion and food blogs reveal the agency, as well as the power of online community building for SAMA women. Religion, culture and gender shape these online discourses.

THE FUTURE OF COSMOPOLITAN CONSUMPTION AND SAMA IDENTITIES

My research shows how Desi blogs and Muslim blogs become sites of narrative making and cultural production for SAMA women. These sites that SAMA women follow change the narrative of what it means to be a Muslim American woman. Since blogs are "under the radar of the public gaze," they are sites of negotiation, resistance, and affirmation (Boy, Uitermark, and Wiersma 2018, 35).

Counterpublics lift up the identity of groups that have been stigmatized, such as women or other minorities. Blogs and social media sites can become counterpublics when they challenge negative stereotypes of South Asian and/or Muslim women, as we see on sites like Brown Girl or Muslim Girl. I expand this understanding by including in my discussion of modest Muslim women, those who veil as well as those who choose not to veil but who still dress modestly. Secondly, I argue that these media are sites of negotiation, definition, and debate around what is religious or fashionable but also what is political.

As I mention in chapter 3, blogs like Brown Girl and Muslim Girl are places where SAMA women can construct and negotiate their multiple ethnic, religious, classed, and gendered identities, affirm their communities, and resist harmful and toxic messages. Even more so, these can also be sites of solidarity and resistance to oppressive politics including resistance to Trump-era policies around ICE, the Muslim-ban, or silence in response to state-sanctioned racial violence.

Social media, including blogs and Instagram, is important for studying marginalized identities. Consumption is linked to identity for SAMA women through halal food and modest fashion. Through seeking to understanding how cultural, social, and economic capital shape these consumption patterns as they are filtered through global and cosmopolitan consumption, we begin to see how consumption must also be interpreted through a global, political, and intersectional lens. We can continue to understand how SAMA women use Instagram and social media for consumption but also political consumption and resistance.

In the Trump era, where minorities were hyper-surveilled, counterpublics like Black Twitter, Muslim or South Asian blogs were even more important for understanding stigmatized identities. Since COVID-19, bloggers on Muslim Girl and Brown Girl have addressed these increasing disparities. Additionally, after the murders of Ahmed Arbery and George Floyd, both sites have aligned Muslim solidarity with Black Lives Matter (BLM), South Asian activism, and Black Americans; further, these blogs are also beginning to address the anti-Black racism in their own South Asian and Muslim communities. These alliances are not always clearly understood in physical spaces but are often coded in visuals such as BLM t-shirts worn by the microcelebrities or other signals on Instagram. Similarly to how the #MeToo movement addressed rape culture by making women's real experiences visible, SAMA women are using social media to make their realities visible and simultaneously challenge the misogynist and xenophobic rhetoric which have attempted to silence or erase them. This is evidenced online in multiple intersectional ways that they build solidarity with South Asian and Muslim immigrants, and, more recently, with immigrants and Black Lives Matter.

POSTSCRIPT

The end of this project in January of 2021 coincided with Kamala Harris's inauguration as vice president of the United States. At this time, as in the year leading up to the election, Harris faces ample public scrutiny—and many of her experiences reflect the same sorts of challenges faced by the SAMA women described in this book. Kamala Harris is also negotiating multiple identities, including her biracial identity, her identity as a female politician, and her upper-class identity. She's the daughter of an Indian Hindu mother and a Black Christian father, and she is also the wife of a white Jewish husband. As she balances these multiple identities, she also must contend with how she is perceived by the white American public.

As with many female politicians in the United States, even in 2021, Vice President Harris's appearance and consumption choices have been featured prominently during her time in the public eye. Her clothing, her appearance, and the food she eats and prepares have all been part of her public image as she faces questions about her authentic ethnic identities (her Blackness and South Asian-ness) and her femininity. This project further illuminates how and why women's public consumption is under scrutiny. Like women throughout our society, and like the SAMA women in this study, how Kamala Harris consumes "feminine" goods like clothing and fashion is understood to communicate her identities to the public. This book gives us perspective to examine how race, class, gender, religion, and politics intersect in her consumption practices.

Similar to the upper-middle-class SAMA women presented in this book, Kamala Harris practices cosmopolitan consumption from her clothing to her shoes. Moreover, her clothing is often selected to signal and blend together her membership in certain groups. Harris's designer outfits for inauguration day were both created by Black fashion designers. For her swearing in, she wore a purple Christopher Rogers coat over a matching dress with pearls. Purple is a coded color. It can be traced back to the Byzantine Era, when it was considered majestic. For suffragettes, purple signals "loyalty and hope." Purple—the mixing of red and blue—has also been viewed as a color of unity. Like Harris, Shirley Chisolm wore purple during her presidential campaign. (*Newsweek*). On inauguration evening, she chose to wear a sequin cocktail dress with a floor length overcoat designed by Sergio Hudson. The pearls were a nod to her Alpha Kappa Alpha sorority. AKA is one of the nation's oldest Black sororities, and she was an active member in her time at Howard University. The founders are referred to as "twenty pearls," and every new member is gifted a necklace of twenty pearls (Smithsonian, January 25, 2021).

Overall her wardrobe choices can be read through an intersectional lens signaling her racial identity, commitment to women's rights, and class identity. In her November acceptance speech in Delaware, she wore a white pantsuit. Like the pearls, the woman's pant suit has an important history coded with women's rights. The color white has historically been associated with the suffragettes. Shirley Chisolm wore white when she became the first Black woman in Congress in 1968.

Perhaps most visibly, Kamala Harris is most well-known for her choice in footwear, best exemplified by her Chuck Taylor All Stars Converse sneakers. Though it began as a basketball shoe, it became associated with counter culture, popular culture, and even sneaker couture. The history of the Converse has been associated with rebellion, resistance, and authenticity from Jesse Owens in the 1936 Olympic Games to popular culture icons like James Dean to Kurt Cobain. Kamala Harris's choice of the Converse shoe signals an accessibility but also an embracing of popular culture.

For its February 2021 issue, *Vogue* released a now infamous photo of Kamala Harris dressed in a black pantsuit, wearing sneakers, with her skin washed out by harsh lighting. Though the fashion team that worked with her to put together the *Vogue* cover was predominantly Black, the magazine experienced a backlash about the portrayal of the first Black vice president. Why, people wanted to know, did they choose a cover where she was dressed and posed so casually? *Vogue* told TODAY that they "felt the more informal image captured Vice President-elect Harris's authentic, approachable nature."[3] The choice to put her in a pantsuit and sneakers, a signature choice she often makes for herself, was a consumption choice meant to do identity work for her. On the one hand, the suit is professional, political, and powerful—and the choice of pants over a skirt or dress nods to the Pantsuit Nation group that emerged during the previous election in support of Hilary Clinton. On the other hand, the Chuck Taylors are casual and "approachable," possibly an attempt to counteract perceptions about her racial heritage or to moderate the powerful image, as is often expected from women. Unfortunately, the more casual look and posing was seen trivializing her professional role as the first South Asian and Black vice president: "Critics took aim at the lighting and styling, calling the image 'washed out' and asserting that the casual outfit was not appropriate for a historic magazine cover of the first woman and woman of color elected as Vice President of the United States" (cnn.com, Jacqui Palumbo, January 12, 2021). How she was dressed clearly resonated with the identities she was trying to claim.

Negotiating identities through consumption, though in part an internal process of choosing how to honor and observe different identities, can be fraught if the groups a woman is trying to signal to do not receive those signals as intended. The cover was not received well by certain publics. In particular, the South Asian community, both abroad in India and in the United States, and the Black community domestically associated the poor lighting with a long history of skin lightening and colorism in these parts of the world. This context exacerbated concerns over whether the cover choice failed to make Harris appear vice presidential. Just as the SAMA women that I studied have to navigate the tension between the ideals of their South Asian or religious identities and the values and perceptions of the general American public to which they also belong, Kamala Harris has been publicly negotiating tensions between her racial, gender, and political identities through fashion consumption.

Kamala Harris also has demonstrated her authenticity as South Asian through her cooking segment on cooking dosas with Mindy Kaling (*Guardian*, 2019). By participating in this cooking video, Harris signaled her Indian diaspora identity. Both she and Kaling also shared their South Indian heritage as they spoke about their fondness for specific foods like idli, a rice cake common in Chennai (the region her mother is from), and daal. Harris and Kaling both trace their ancestry to the same neighborhood in Chennai, India.

Other public figures also signal their Indian and American identities through food. Congresswoman Pramila Jayapal cooked paneer tikka in honor of Harris the eve of the election. She tweeted, "Compulsive, night-before-election activity: make comfort food. That's paneer tikka tonight, in honor of electing #KamalaHarris Veep tomorrow since she just said on Instagram her favorite North Indian food is any kind of tikka." Indian social media users went back and forth debating the authenticity and the imagery used by Jayapal, another important example of how food is used as an indicator of ethnic and gendered immigrant identity.

More recently, Padma Lakshmi cooked tamarind rice in honor of Kamala Harris. *The Indian Times* abroad ran a piece about Kamala Harris's favorite Indian dishes as "really good sambar" and "any kind of tikka" (*The Indian Times*, November 8, 2020). Sambar is a South Asian soup like the South Indian dish usually served with dosa. Tikka usually refers to chicken tikka and is a North Indian food commonly found in most South Asian American restaurants, though it is not a South Indian dish. Negotiating South Asian heritage with middle-class and gendered identities through the preparation and sharing of food was also a common practice amongst the SAMA women in my research.

Often perceived as trivial or fanciful, consumption practices confer identity for women. Moreover, consumption choices are not passively adopted, but rather they are actively constructed to blend sometimes competing identities. These competing identities are often shaped by race, class, gender, and religion, especially for racialized women. As this book has demonstrated, consumption patterns can be a window into the ways in which women are reinforcing their belonging in their South Asian, Muslim, and American communities and their senses of self.

NOTES

1. Shepard Fairey created the protest poster. Munira Ahmed is the face of the woman in hijab. More are artnet.com (January 20, 2017).

2. Cooperhewitt.org. "Major Exhibition Explores the Modest Fashion Industry's Rise."

3. Citation: https://www.today.com/popculture/kamala-harris-vogue-cover-prompts-backlash-over-lighting-styling-t205448.

References

Abarca, Meredith. 2004. "Authentic or Not, It's Original." *Food and Foodways* 12: 1–25.
Abarca, Meredith E. 2006. *Voices in the Kitchen: Views of Food and the World from Working-Class Mexican and Mexican American Women.* College Station, TX: Texas A&M Press.
Abdullah, Fatima. 2019. *Always keeping Palestine.* November 12. Accessed June 29, 2021.
———. 2018. *Gaza Bleeds.* May 26. Accessed June 29, 2021.
———. 2019. *I Still Can't Believe We're . . .* May 31. Accessed June 29, 2021.
Abidin, Crystal. 2015. "Commiunicative Intimacies: Influencers and Perceived Interconnectedness." *Ada: A Journal of Gender, New Media & Technology* 8: 1–17.
Ahmed, Leila. 2012. *Women and Gender in Islam: Historical Roots of a Modern Debate.* New Haven, CT: Yale University Press.
Albarcha, Summer. 2012. *@summeralbarcha.* August 18. Accessed June 29, 2021.
———. 2004. *Accessorizing my abaya with these #posttareeweeh late night snacks.* July 21. Accessed June 29, 2021.
———. 2012. *Possible inspiration for your Eid outfit.* August 18. Accessed June 21, 2021.
Al-hibri, Aziza. 1982. "Women and Islam." *Journal of Women's Studies International Forum* (Pergamon Press) Special Monograph Issue.
Ali, Kecia. 2006. *Sexual Ethics and Islam: Feminist Reflections on Qur'an, Hadith, and Jurisprudence.* Oxford: Pergamon Press.
Alia, Maria. 2017. *full@lorealmakeup.* November 13. Accessed June 29, 2021.
———. 2019. *My Dad Grew up in a Palestinian Refugee Camp in Lebanon.* July 19. Accessed June 26, 2021.
Appadurai, Arjun. 1986. *The Social Life of Things: Commodities in Cultural Perspective.* Cambridge: Cambridge University Press.
Armanios, Febe, and Bogac A. Ergene. 2018. *Halal Food: A History.* Oxford: Oxford University Press.

Avakian, Arelene. 2005. "Shish Kebab Americans?: Food and the Construction and Maintenance of Ethnic and Gender Identities among Aremenian American Feminists." In *From Betty Crocker to Feminist Food Stuides: Critical Perspectives on Women and Food*, edited by Arelene Avakian and Barbara Haber, 257-280. Amherst: University of Massachusetts Press.

Avakian, Arlene. 1997. *Through the Kitchen Window*. Boston: Beacon Press.

Baulch, Emma, and Alila Pramiyanti. 2018. "Hijabers on Instagram: Using Visual Social Media to Construct the Ideal Muslim Woman." *Social Media + Society* 1–15.

BBC. 2017. *This is what it's like to wear hijiab and live in Donald Trump's America*. April 7. Accessed June 30, 2021. https://www.bbc.com/news/newsbeat-29504837.

Beagan, Brenda, Gwen E. Chapman, Andrea D'Sylva, and B. Raewyn Bassett. 2008. "'It's Just Easier for Me to Do It: Rationalizing the Family Division of Foodwork." *Sociology* 42 (4): 653–671.

Bhabha, Homi. 1994. *The Location of Culture*. New York: Routledge.

Bhachu, Parminder. 1995. "New Cultural Forms and Transnational Asian Women: Culture, Class and Consumption among British Asian women in the Diaspora." In *Nation and Migration: The Politics of Space in the South Asian Diaspora*, edited by Peter van der Veer, 56-85. Philadelphia: University of Pennsylvania Press.

Bharde, Saleha. 2018. *9 Quick & Healthy Recipes for the Time-Strapped Woman*. February 1. Accessed June 29, 2021. https://blog.hautehijab.com/post/quick-healthy-recipes-for-the-time-strapped-woman.

Bhutani, Saumya. 2014. *5 Reasons We Need "The Mindy Project."* July 15. Accessed June 29, 2021. https://browngirlmagazine.com/2014/07/need-the-mindy-project/.

Bourdieu, Pierre. 1984. *Distinction: A Social Critique of the Judgement of Taste*. Cambridge: Harvard University Press.

Bowen, Sarah, Joslyn Brenton, and Sinnika Elliot. 2019. *Pressure Cooker: Why Home Cooking Won't Solve Our Problems and What We Can Do About It*. New York: Oxford University Press.

Boy, John D., Justus Uitermark, and Laila Wiersma. 2018. "Trending #hijabfashion: Using Big Data to Study Religion at the Online-Urban Interface." *Nordic Journal of Religion and Society* 31 (1): 22–40.

Cairns, Kate, and Josee Johnston. 2015. *Food and Femininity*. New York: Bloomsbury.

Cairns, Kate, Josee Jonston, and Norah MacKendrick. 2013. "Feeding the 'Organic Child': Mothering Through Ethical Consumption." *Journal of C/onsumer Culture* 13 (2): 97–118.

Carrington, Christopher. 1998. *No Place Like Home: Relationships and Family Life Among Lesbians and Gay Men*. Chicago: University of Chicago.

Chandan, Rema. 2017. *Bollywood's Unfair and Ugly Obsession with Dark Skin Color*. March 2. Accessed June 29, 2021. https://browngirlmagazine.com/2017/03/bollywoods-unfair-and-ugly-obsession-with-dark-skin-color/.

Chatterji, Joya[Washbrook, David, ed. 2013. *Routledge Handbook of the South Asian Diaspora*. New York: Routledge.

Chhabra, Deepak, Woojin Lee, Shengnan Zhao, and Karla Scott. 2013. "Marketing of Ethnic Food Experiences: Authentication Analysis of Indian Cuisine Abroad." *Journal of Heritage Tourism* 8 (2-3): 145–157.

Chin, Elizabeth. 2001. *Purchasing Power: Black Kids and American Consumer Culture.* Minneapolis: University of Minnesota Press.

Cinotto, Simone. 2014. *Making Italian America: Consumer Culture and the Production of Ethnic Identities.* New York: Fordham University Press.

Collins, Patricia Hill. 1990. *Black Feminist Thought: Knowledge, Consciousness and the Politics of Empowerment.* Boston: Routledge.

Collins, Patricia Hill. 2015. "Intersectionality's Definitional Dilemmas." *Annual Review of Sociology* 41: 1–20.

Collins, Patricia Hill, and Valerie Chepp. 2013. "Intersectionality." In *The Oxford Handbook of Gender and Politics*, edited by Georgina Waylen, Karen Celis, Johanna Kantola and S. Laurel Weldon, 57-87. New York: Oxford University Press.

Cooke, Miriam. 2007. "The Muslim Women." *Contemporary Islam* 1 (2): 139–154.

Counihan, Carole. 2004. *Around the Tuscan Table: Food, Family and Gender in the Twentieth Century.* New York: Routledge.

Crane, Diane. 2000. *Fashion and Its Social Agendas: Class, Gender and Identity in Clothing.* Chicago: University of Chicago.

Crenshaw, Kimberle. 1989. "Demarginalizing the Intersection of Race and Sex: A Black Feminist Critique of Antidiscrimination Doctrine, Feminist Theory and Antiracist Politics." *University of Chicago Legal Forum* (1, Article 8).

Davila, Arelene. 2001. *Latinos, Inc.: The Marketing and Making of a People.* Berkeley: University of California Press.

Davis, Fred. 1992. *Fashion, Culture, and Identity.* Chicago: University of Chicago Press.

de Camargo Heck, Marina. 2003. "Adapting and Adopting: The Migrating Recipe." In *The Recipe Reader: Narratives, Contexts, Traditions*, by Janet Forster and Laurel Floyd, 205-218. London: Ashgate.

de Perthuis, Karen, and Fosie Findlay. 2019. "How Fashion Travels: The Fashionable Ideal in the Age of Instagram." *Fashion Theory* 23 (2): 1–24.

DeSoucey, Michaela. 2016. *Contested Tastes: Foie Gras and the Politics of Food.* Princeton: Princeton University Press.

DeVault, Marjorie L. 1991. *Feeding the Family: The Social Organization of Caring as Gendered Work.* Chicago: University of Chicago Press.

Diner, Hasia R. 2003. *Hungering for America: Italian, Irish and Jewish Foodways in the Age of Migration.* Cambridge: Harvard.

Donner, Henrike. 2008. *Domestic Goddesses: Maternity, Globalization and Middle-Class Identity in Contemporary India.* Hampshire: Ashgate.

Du Boise, W.E.B. 1903. *The Souls of Black Folk.* Chicago: A.C. McClurg & Co.

Dufy, Brooke Erin, and Emily Hund. 2015. "'Having It All' on Social Media: Entrepreneurial Femininity and Self-Branding Among Fashion Bloggers." *Social Media + Society* 1 (2): 1–11.

Ebaugh, Helen Rose, and Janet Saltzman Chafetz. 2000. *Religion and the New Immigrants: Continuities and Adaptations in Immigrant Congregations.* Walnut Creek: Alta Mira Press.

Eckert, Stine, and Kalyani Chadha. 2013. "Muslim Bloggers in Germany: An Emerging Counterpublic." *Media, Culture & Society* 35 (8): 926–942.

Elturk, Melanie. 2015. *A Hijabi's Guide to Eating Healthy & Melanie's Secrets to Staying Trim.* April 22. Accessed June 29, 2021. https://blog.hautehijab.com/post/18645825-a-hijabis-guide-to-eating-healthy-melanies-secrets-to-staying-trim.

———. 2021. *Our Story.* Accessed June 29, 2021. https://www.hautehijab.com/pages/our-story.

Ewen, Elizabeth. 1985. *Immigrant Women in the Land of Dollars: Life and Culture on the Lower East Side.* New York: Monthly Review Press.

Forson-Williams, Psyche. 2007. "More Than Just the 'Big Piece of Chicken': The Power of Race, Class, and Food in American Consciousness." In *Food and Culture: A Reader*, edited by Carole Counihan and Penny van Esterik, 121-132. New York: Routledge.

Forson-Williams, Psyche, and Abby Wilkerson. 2011. "Intersectionality and Food Studies." *Food, Culture & Society* 14 (1): 7–28.

Friedberg, Susanne. 2009. *Fresh: A Perishable History.* Cambridge: Harvard University Press.

Gabaccia, Donna. 1998. *You Are What You Eat: Ethnic Food and the Making of Americans.* Cambridge: Harvard University Press.

Garner, Steve, and Saher Selod. 2016. "The Racialization of Muslims: Empirical Studies of Islamophobia." *Critical Sociology* 41 (1): 9–19.

Garner, Steve, and Saher Selod. 2015. "The Radicalization of Muslims: Empirical Studies of Islamophobia." *Critical Sociology* 41 (1): 9–19.

Guha, Ramachandra. 2004. "The Spread of the Salwar." *The Hindu*, October 24. Accessed June 30, 2021. https://www.thehindu.com/todays-paper/tp-features/tp-sundaymagazine/the-spread-of-the-salwar/article28528266.ece.

Gvion, Liora. 2012. *Beyond Hummus and Falafel.* Berkeley: University of California Press.

Habib, Samar. 2016. "LGBT Activism in the Middle East." In *The Wiley Blackwell Encyclopedia of Gender and Sexuality Studies*. Wiley Online Library. doi: https://doi.org/10.1002/9781118663219.wbegss664.

Habib, Samar. 2013. "Sexualities and Queer Studies." In *Women and Islamic Cultures*, edited by Suad Joseph, 37-50. Boston: Brill.

Haddad, Yvonne. 2007. "Post 9/11: Hijab as Icon." *Sociology of Religion* 68 (3): 243–267.

Halter, Marilyn. 2000. *Shopping for Identity: The Marketing of Ethnicity.* New York: Schocken Books.

Hansen, Karen. 2004. "The World in Dress: Anthropological Perspectives on Clothing, Fashion, and Culture." *Annual Review of Anthropology* 33: 369–392.

Haythornwaite, Caroline. 2005. "Social Networks and Internet Connectivity Effects." *Information, Communication & Society* 8 (2): 125–147.

Heldke, Lisa. 2003. *Exotic Appetites: Ruminations of a Food Adventurer.* New York: Routledge.

Hermansen, Marcia. 1991. "Two-Way Acculturation: Muslim Women in America Between Individal Choice (Liminality) and Community Affiliation (Communitas)." In *The Muslims of America*, edited by Yvonne Y. Haddad, 188-201. New York: Oxford University Press.

Hermanssen, Marcia, and Mahruq Khan. 2009. "South Asian Muslim American Girl Power: Structures and Symbols of Control and Self-Expression." *Journal of International Women's Studies* 11 (1): 86–105.

Hochschild, Arlie, and Anne Machung. 1989. *The Second Shift.* New York: Penguin.

hooks, bell. 1981. *Ain't I a Woman: Black Women and Feminism.* Boston: South End Press.

Horowitz, Roger. 2016. *Kosher USA: How Coke Became Kosher and Other Tales of Modern Food.* New York: Columbia University Press.

Jhaish, Zeina. 2019. *7 Palestinian Chefs That Are Doing It For The Culture.* March 15. Accessed June 29, 2021. https://muslimgirl.com/7-palestinian-chefs-that-are-doing-it-for-the-culture/.

Johnston, Josee, and Shyon Baumann. 2009. *Foodies: Democracy and Distinction in the Food Landscape.* New York: Routledge.

———. 2014. *Foodies: Democracy and Distinction in the Gourmet Foodscape.* New York: Routledge.

Julier, Alice. 2013. *Eating Together: Food, Friendship, and Inequality.* Urbana: University of Illinois Press.

Kandiyoti, Deniz. 1988. "Bargaining with Patriarchy." *Gender and Society* 2 (3): 274–290.

Karnani, Aneel. 2007. "Doing Well by Doing Good - Case Study: 'Fair & Lovely' Whitening Cream." *Strategic Management Journal* 28 (13): 1351–1357.

Kavakci, Elif, and Camille R. Kraeplin. 2016. "Religious Beings in Fashionable Bodies: The Online Identity Construction of Hijabi Social Media Personalities." *Media, Culture & Society* 39 (6): 1–19.

Khabeer, Suad Abdul. 2016. *Muslim Cool: Race, Religion, and Hip Hop in the United States.* New York: New York University Press.

Khan, Mahruq F., and Marcia Hermansen. 2008. "Bismillahs, Barbies and Bling; Loyola Girls Studies Conference Report." *American Journal of Islamic Social Sciences* 25 (4): 152–155.

Khan, Mahruq F., and Marcia Hermansen. 2009. "South Asian Muslim American Girl Power: Structures and Symbols of Control and Self-Expression." *Journal of International Women's Studies* 11 (1): 1–20.

Khan, Shehnaz. 1998. "Muslim Women: Negotiations in the Third Space." *Signs: Journal of Women in Culture and Society* 23 (2): 463–494.

Kondo, Marie. 2014. *The Life-Changing Magic of Tidying Up: The Japanese Art of Decluttering and Organizing.* New York: Clarkson Potter/Ten Speed.

Lanham, Lamees. 2017. *8 Health Tips to Beat the Fasting Fatigue During Ramadan.* May 22. Accessed June 29, 2021. https://blog.hautehijab.com/post/health-tips-to-beat-the-fasting-fatigue-this-ramadan.

Lee, Latoya. 2017. "Black Twitter: A Response to Bias in Mainstream Media." *Social Sciences* 6 (1): 1–17.

Lewis, Reina. 2013. "Insider Voices, Changing Practices: Press and Industry Professionals." In *Modest Fashion, Styling Bodies, Mediating Faith*, edited by Reina Lewis, 190-220. London: Tauris.

Lewis, Reina. 2010. "Marketing Muslim Women Marketing Muslim Lifestyle: A New Media." *Journal of Middle East Women's Studies* 6 (3): 58–90.

———. 2015. *Muslim Fashion: Contemporary Style Cultures*. Durham: Duke University Press.

Lu, Shun, and Gary Alan Fine. 1995. "The Presentation of Ethnic Authenticity: Chinese Food as Social Accomplishment." *The Sociological Quarterly* 36 (3): 535–553.

Magpantay, Glenn D. 2016. "The Future of the LGBTQ Asian American and Pacific Islander Community in 2040." *AAPI Nexus: Policy, Practice and Community* 14 (2): 33–48.

Mahmood, Saba. 2012. *Politics of Piety: The Islamic Revival and the Feminist Subject*. Princeton: Princeton University Press.

———. 2005. *Politics of Piety: The Islamic Revival and the Feminist Subject*. Princeton: Princeton University Press.

Maira, Sumaina. 2002. *Desis In The House: Indian American Youth Culture in Ne York*. Philadelphia: Temple University Press.

Majumdar, Samirah. 2018. *5 Facts About Religion in India*. June 29. Accessed June 30, 2021. https://www.pewresearch.org/fact-tank/2018/06/29/5-facts-about-religion-in-india/.

Mani, Bakirathi. 2002. "Undressing the Diaspora." In *South Asian Women in the Diaspora*, edited by Nirmal Puwar and Parvati Raghuram, 117-136. Oxford: Bloomsbury.

Mankekur, Purnima. 2002. "'India Shopping': Indian Grocery Stores and Transnational Configurations of Belonging." *Ethnos* 67 (1): 75–97.

Mannur, Anita. 2009. *Culinary Fictions: Food in South Asian Diasporic Culture*. Philadelphia: Temple University Press.

Marwick, Alice E. 2015. "Instafame: Luxury Selfies in the Attention Economy." *Pulic Culture* 137–160.

McIntosh, Wm. Alex, and Mary Zey. 1989. "Women as Gatekeepers of Food Consumption: A Sociological Critique." *Food and Foodways* 3 (4): 317–332.

Mejova, Yelena, Youcef Benkhadda, and Khairani. 2017. "#Halal Culture on Instagram." *Frontiers in Digital Humanities* 4. Accessed June 29, 2021. https://www.frontiersin.org/article/10.3389/fdigh.2017.00021.

Mernissi, Fatima. 1991. *The Veil and the Male Elite: A Feminist Interpretation of Women's Rights in Islam*. Translated by Mary Jo Lakeland. New York: Addison-Wesley.

Miller, Daniel, and Susanne Kuchler. 2005. *Clothing as Material Culture*. London: Bloomsbury.

Mir, Shabana. 2014. *Muslim American Women on Campus: Undergraduate Social Life and Identity*. Chapel Hill: University of North Carolina Press.

Moors, Annelise. 2015. "Fashion and Anti-Fashion: The Aesthetics of Fully Covering in the Netherlands." In *Islamic Fashion and Anti-Fashion: New Perspectives from Europe and America*, edited by Emma Tarlo and Annelies Moors, 241-259. New York: Bloomsbury Academic.

Mubarakah, Ibrahim. 2013. *a hijabi can . . . be a personal trainer.* January 12. Accessed June 29, 2021. https://www.blog.hijabican.com/a-hijabi-can-be-a-personal-trainer/.

Murcott, Anne. 1986. "Opening the 'Black Box': Food, Eating, and Household Relationships." *Sosioaaliliaaketieteellinen Aikakauslehti* 23: 85–92.

Murcott, Anne. 1995. "Social Influences on Food Choice and Dietary Change: A Sociological Attitude." *Proceedings of the Nutrition Society* 54 (3): 729–735.

Narayan, Anjana, and Bandana Purkayastha. 2009. *Living Our Religions: South Asian Hindu and Muslim Women Narrate Their Experiences.* Sterling: Kumarian Press.

Narayan, Uma. 1997. *Dislocating Cultures: Identities, Traditions, and Third World Feminism.* New York: Routledge.

Nene, Chhaye. 2016. *'Miss Moti' Author Kripa Josi on Promoting Positive Body Image Through Her Comics.* August 19. Accessed June 29, 2021. https://browngirlmagazine.com/2016/09/miss-moti-author-kripa-joshi-on-promoting-positive-body-image-through-her-comics/.

Norris, Pippa. 2004. "Bridging and Bonding in Online Communities." *Society Online: The Internet in Context* 1 (1): 19–39.

Nouser, Mariam. 2019. *How I Use My Sense of Style to Challenge Stereotypes About My Being.* April 3. Accessed June 29, 2021. https://muslimgirl.com/how-i-use-my-sense-of-style-to-challenge-stereotypes-about-my-being/.

Ocampo, Anthony C., and Daniel Soodjinda. 2016. "Invisible Asian Americans: The Intersection of Sexuality, Race, and Education Among Gay Asian Americans." *Race and Ethnicity in Education* 19 (3): 480–499.

Parasecoli, Fabio. 2014. "Food, Identity, and Cultural Reproduction in Immigrant Communities." *Social Research* 81 (2): 415–439.

Peterson, Kristin M. 2020. "The Unruly, Loud and Intersectional Muslim Woman: Interpreting the Aesthetic Styles of Islamic Fashion Images on Instagram." *International Journal of Communication* 14: 1194–1213.

Peterson, Richard A., and Roger M. Kern. 1996. "Changing Highbrow Taste: From Snow to Omnivores." *American Sociological Review* 61 (5): 900–907.

Pilcher, Jeffrey M. 2012. *Planet Taco: A Global History of Mexican Food.* Oxford: Oxford University Press.

Power, Elaine, Barbara Parker, Jennifer Brady, and Susan Belyea,. 2019. *Feminist Food Studies: International Perspectives.* Toronto: Women's Press/Canadian Scholar's Press.

Prosterman, Leslie. 1984. "Food and Celebration: A Kosher Caterer as Mediator of Communal Traditions." In *Ethnic and Regional Foodways in the United States: The Performance of Group Identity*, edited by Linda Keller Brown and Kay Mussell, 127-142. Knoxville: University of Tennessee Press.

Purkayastha, Bandana. 2012. "Intersectionality in a Transnational World." *Gender and Society* 26 (1): 55–66.

Pyke, Karen D., and Denise L. Johnson. 2003. "Asian American Women and Racialized Femininities: 'Doing' Gender Across Cultural Worlds." *Gender and Society* 17 (1): 33–53.

Radwan, Amina. 2019. *Here's Why I'm Done Apologizing for Not Being a Stick Figure.* March 19. Accessed June 29, 2021. https://muslimgirl.com/heres-why-im-done-apologizing-for-not-being-a-stick-figure/.

Rangaswamy, Padma. 2000. *Namaste America: Indian Immigrants in an American Metropolis.* University Park: Pennsylvania State University Press.

Ray, Krishnendu. 2018. "Culinary Difference: The Difference It Makes." *Notes on the Field* 5 (2). Accessed June 29, 2021. https://gradfoodstudies.org/2018/12/11/culinary-difference/.

Ray, Krishnendu. 2012. "Global Flows, Local Bodies: Dreams of Pakistani Grill in Manhattan." In *Curried Cultures: Globalization, Food, and South Asia*, edited by Krishnendu Ray and Tulasi Srinivas, 175-195. Berkeley: University of California Press.

———. 2016. *The Ethnic Restauranteur.* London: Bloomsbury.

———. 2004. *The Migrant's Table: Meals and Memories in Bengali-American Households.* Philadelphia: Temple University Press.

Read, Je'nan, and J.P. Bartkowski. 2000. "To Veil or Not To Veil?: A Case Study of Identity Negotiation among Muslim Women in Austin, Texas." *Gender and Society* 14 (3): 395–417.

Rehman, Shehzeen. 2008. *Haj Mubarak.* August 21.

———. 2019. *Making an average day kinda fancy.* July 15.

Sehmi, Sejal. 2017. *Examining Bharti Singh's Prominence Amidst Bollywood's Fat-Shaming Culture.* April 26. Accessed June 29, 2021. https://browngirlmagazine.com/2017/04/examining-bharti-singh-prominence-bollywood-fat-shaming/.

Selod, Saher. 2018. *Forever Suspect.* New Brunswick: Rutgers University Press.

Sengupta, Jayanta. 2013. "Indian Food in the USA: Adapting to Culinary Eclecticism." In *Routledge Handbook of the South Asian Diaspora*, edited by Joya Chatterji and David Washbrook, 400-408. New York: Routledge.

Shankar, Shalini. 2015. *Advertising Diversity: Producing Language and Ethnicity in American Advertising.* Durham: Duke University Press.

———. 2008. *Desi Land: Teen Culture, Class, and Success in Silicon Valley.* Chapel Hill: Duke University Press.

Sharma, Ursula. 1986. *Women's Work, Class, and the Urban Household: A Study of Shimla, North India.* London: Tavistock Publications.

Shirazi, Faegheh. 2016. *Brand Islam: The Marketing and Commodification of Piety.* Austin: University of Texas Press.

———. 2016. *Brand Islam: The Marketing and Commodity of Peity.* Austin: University of Texas Press.

Siraj, Asifa. 2011. "Meanings of Modesty and the Hijab Amongst Muslim Women in Glasgow, Scotland." *Gender, Place & Culture* 18 (6): 716–731.

Srinivas, Tulasi. 2006. "'As Mother Made It': The Cosmopolitan Indian Family, 'Authentic' Indian Food and the Construction of Cultural Utopia." *International Journal of Sociology of the Family* 32 (2): 191–221.

Suleiman, Hawthar. 2020. *About Us.* August 1. Accessed June 29, 2021. https://www.hijabican.com/pages/about-us.
Tarlo, Emma. 2010. *Visibly Muslim: Fashion, Politics, Faith.* New York: Bloomsbury.
Ternikar, Farha. 2010. "Teaching and Learning Guide for: Hijab and the Abrahamic Traditions." *Sociology Compass* 4 (8): 690–693.
Theophano, Janet. 2003. *Eat My Words: Reading Women's Lives Through the Cookbooks They Wrote.* Baltimore: Johns Hopkins University Press.
Vallianatos, Helen, and Kim Raine. 2008. "Consuming Food and Constructing Identities among Arabic and South Asian Indian Women." *Food, Culture & Society* 11 (3): 355–373.
Veblen, Thorsten. 1899. *The Theory of the Leisure Class.* New York: Macmillan.
———. 1953. *The Theory of the Leisure Class: An Economic Study of Institutions, The Mentor Edition.* New York: Macmillan.
Waninger, Kelsey. 2015. "The Veiled Identity: Hijabistas, Instagram and Branding in the Online Islamic Fashion Industry." *Master's Thesis.* Georgia State University.
Warren, Saskia. 2019. "#YourAverageMuslim: Ruptural Geopolitics of British Muslim Women's Media and Fashion." *Political Geography* 69: 118–127.
Warren, Saskia. 2018. "Placing Faith in Creative Labour: Muslim Women and Digital Media Work in Britain." *Geoforum* 97: 1–9.
Weber, Max. 1958. *From Max Weber: Essays in Sociology.* New York: Oxford University Press.
Weller, Daniel L., and David Turkon. 2014. "Contextualizing the Immigrant Experience: The Role of Food and Foodways in Identity Maintenance and Formation for First-and Second-Generation Latinos in Ithaca, New York." *Ecology, Food and Nutrition* 54 (1): 57–73.
West, Candace, and Don Zimmerman. 1987. "Doing Gender." *Gender and Society* 1 (2): 125–151.
West, Candace, and Sarah Fenstermaker. 1997. "Doing Difference." *Gender and Society* 9 (1): 8–37.
Williams, Rhys H., and Gira Vashi. 2007. "Hijab and American Muslim Women: Creating the Space for Autonomous Selves." *Sociology of Religion* 68 (2): 269–287.
Williams-Forson, Psyche. 2006. *Building Houses Out of Chicken Legs: Black Women, Food & Power.* Chapel Hill: University of North Carolina Press.
Zanoni, Elizabeth. n.d. *Migrant Marketplaces: Food and Italians in North and South America.* Champaign: University of Illinois Press.
Zukin, Sharon. 2004. *Point of Purchase.* New York: Routledge.

Index

Abarca, Meredith, 23
Abdullah, Fatima Ali: on discrimination, 90; as influencer, 89–90; Al-Sadek compared with, 91
African Americans: Chin on, 6–7; consumption by, 6–7; SAMA women compared to, 9; on social media, 71
Albarcha, Summer, 91–92
Arab Muslim women, 62
Armanios, Febe, 21
authenticity: class and, 28; consumer culture indicating, 10; cultural capital of, 23; in fashion, 47; of food, 10, 11, 22; Harris demonstrating, 106; health contrasted with, 31; Heldke on, 22; identity and, 17; SAMA women proving, 9, 14, 25, 27; white people assessing, 20, 23

beauty standards: racialization of, 83; thinness in, 77–78
Bhabha, Homi, 10
big box chains, 38–39
Black Lives Matter, 79, 81
Bollywood, 83, 84–85
Bourdieu, Pierre: on cultural capital, 5; on status, 46
Brand Islam (Shirazi), 55

Brown Girl: Instagram compared to, 87; Muslim Girl compared with, 103; patriarchal norms addressed by, 86; SAMA women represented through, 82–83

Chandan, Rema, 83–84
Chicago, 13–14
children: SAMA women impacted by, 32–33; socialization of, 33, 44
Chin, Elizabeth, 6–7
Chisolm, Shirley, 105
colorism, 83–84
community: consumption creating, viii; LGBTQ, 85; through shopping, 99; social media creating, 70–71
conspicuous consumption, 5; hijab and, 68; identity expressed by, 40, 58; status indicated by, 97
consumer culture: authenticity indicating, 10; Davila emphasizing, 7, 45
consumption: by African Americans, 6–7; community created by, viii; Du Bois on, 45; fashion in, 15; Freidberg on, 37; identity through, 18, 48–49, 98, 105–6; of luxury items, 51; of organic foods, 37–38; political opinion conveyed by, 87; religion

framing, 21, 72; by SAMA women, 2, 12, 13–14; on social media, 15; status shaped by, 65; Veblen on, 4–5
culinary consumption: big box chains influenced by, 38–39; cultural consumption indicated by, 27–28; DeVault on, 26, 27, 29, 34; Gabaccia on, 18; on Haute Hijab, 78–79; identity through, 14–15; Narayan on, 19; nostalgia and, 23–24; packaged food in, 24–25; Ray on, 22; religion influencing, 29, 34–35, 79; by SAMA women, 17, 30, 32, 38; Srinivas on, 25
cultural capital: of authenticity, 23; Bourdieu on, 5; culinary consumption indicating, 27–28; of hijab, 60; of immigrants, 64; of South Asian food, 21–22

Davila, Arlene: consumer culture emphasized by, 7, 45; on ethnic marketing, 7; on Latinos, 7
De Camargo Heck, M., 28
Desi. *See* South Asian Muslim American women (SAMA)
designer clothing, 78
DeVault, Marjorie, 26, 27, 29, 34
dietary restriction: of SAMA women, 34–35, 39; in socialization, 35
discrimination: Abdullah on, 90; colorism and, 84; against hijab, 2; Instagram challenging, 104; Nouser on, 80; SAMA women impacted by, 72, 87, 103, 104; on social media, 94; thinness and, 81; under Trump administration, 97–98
double consciousness, 4
Du Bois, W.E.B., 2, 70; on consumption, 45; on rationalization, 48

Ergene, Bogac, 21
ethnic marketing, 7

Facebook, 50
Fairey, Shepard, 98
fashion: authenticity in, 47; in consumption, 15; hijab in, 70; identity through, 101; of Khan, 1; modesty norms impacting, 61, 102–3; religion impacting, 43, 57; for SAMA women, 16n1, 41, 45–46; Shirazi on, 55; shopping for, 60, 64; status indicated by, 44–45; tradition preserved through, 100
Feeding the Family (DeVault), 26, 29
food: authenticity of, 10, 11, 22; identity through, 28; in intersectionality, 18–19, 26, 29; Islam and, 79; packaged, 24–25; on social media, 69; South Asian, 21–22; tradition through, 99. *See also* organic foods
food colonialism, 20
Freidberg, Susanne, 37
Fresh (Freidberg), 37

Gabaccia, Donna, 18
gender: Gest on, 52; in Islam, 75; makeup indicating, 63; modesty norms and, 69; patriarchal norms and, 68, 85; on social media, 65, 76; wardrobe representing, 52; Zimmerman on, 52

halal cooking: as clean, 36, 37; in Islam, 34–36; by SAMA women, 2, 21; shopping for, 31
Halal Food (Armanios, Ergene), 21
Harris, Kamala: authenticity demonstrated by, 106; identity of, 104–5; Lakshmi honoring, 107; wardrobe of, 105
hate crimes, vii
Haute Hijab: culinary consumption on, 78–79; luxury items on, 78
Heldke, Lisa: on authenticity, 22; food colonialism described by, 20
high-end restaurants, 21–22

hijab: conspicuous consumption and, 68; cultural capital of, 60; discrimination against, 2; Fairey depicting, 98; in fashion, 70; hate crimes and, vii; hoodjab contrasted with, 56; in Islam, 62–63, 77; as luxury items, 59, 74; with makeup, 63; in modesty norms, 47–48, 62, 64, 68, 100–101; patriarchal norms and, 54–55; religious identity marked by, 1, 61; SAMA women wearing, 43, 54, 55–56; status influenced by, 55; triple consciousness on, 62; Trump administration influencing, 90
Hijabican, 77
H&M, 59
homophobia, 85
hoodjab, 56

identity: authenticity and, 17; conspicuous consumption expressing, 40, 58; through consumption, 18, 48–49, 98, 105–6; culinary consumption expressing, 14–15; through fashion, 101; food expressing, 28; of Harris, 104–5; hijab marking, 1; on Instagram, 86; Miller on, 46; patriarchal norms constructing, 99; salwar kameez indicating, 93–94; shopping forming, 6; social media defining, 67; Trump administration impacting, 62, 71; wardrobe and, 44, 51
immigrants: Bhabha on, 10; cultural capital of, 64; religion indicated by, 36; Srinivas on, 10
Indian people, vii, 13, 24
influencers: Abdullah as, 89–90; Rehman as, 94; SAMA women as, 67; on social media, 15–16; status used by, 87
Instagram: Albarcha on, 91–92; Brown Girl compared to, 87; discrimination challenged on, 104; identity on, 86; Marwick on, 75; modesty norms on, 86–88; political opinion on, 89; religion revealed by, 102; Al-Sadek on, 88–89; SAMA women on, 75, 95; status on, 68–69
intersectionality: in food, 18–19, 26, 29; in transnational feminism, 3; Williams-Forson on, 3
invisible labor: patriarchal norms and, 33–34; of SAMA women, 32
Islam: food and, 79; gender in, 75; halal cooking in, 34–36; hijab in, 62–63, 77; Khabeer on, 8–9; LGBTQ community and, 85; social media interpreting, 74

Jayapal, Pramila, 106–7
Jhaish, Zeina, 81

Kaling, Mindy, 106
Khabeer, Suad, 8–9
Khan, Junnah, 1

Lakshmi, Padma, 107
Latinos: Davila on, 7; SAMA women contrasted with, 11
Lee, Latoya, 71
lengha, vii
LGBTQ community, 85
luxury items: consumption of, 51; on Haute Hijab, 78; hijab as, 59, 74; SAMA women buying, 58; status indicated by, 88–89

makeup: gender indicated by, 63; hijab with, 63; modesty norms and, 57
marriage, vii
Marwick, Alice, 75
Michigan, 65n1
Miller, Daniel, 46
Mir, Shabana, 53
model minority, 11
modesty norms: designer clothing following, 78; fashion impacted by, 61, 102–3; gender and, 69; hijab in, 47–48, 62, 64, 68, 100–101; on

Instagram, 86–88; makeup and, 57; Mir on, 53; politics of, 90; in religion, 41, 53, 76; Al-Sadek on, 88; of SAMA women, 57, 76; in socialization, 56–58; on social media, 73, 74, 95; in third space identities, 81; wardrobe influenced by, 58
mothers: organic foods prioritized by, 39; SAMA women as, 37
Muslim Cool (Khabeer), 8
Muslim Girl: Black Live Matter addressed by, 81; Brown Girl compared with, 103; third space identities and, 80–82

Narayan, Uma, 19
9/11: SAMA women impacted by, 4; triple consciousness after, 12
nostalgia: culinary consumption and, 23–24; wardrobe influenced by, 61
Nouser, Mariam, 80

organic foods: consumption of, 37–38; mothers prioritizing, 39; status signaled by, 40; zebiha with, 36

Pakistani people, vii, 13
Palestinian people, 90
patriarchal norms: Brown Girl dressing, 86; gender influenced by, 68, 85; hijab and, 54–55; identity constructed by, 99; invisible labor and, 33–34; rationalization and, 45, 80; SAMA women impacted by, 33–34
Point of Purchase (Zukin), 5
political opinion: consumption conveying, 87; on Instagram, 89; of modesty norms, 90; of Palestinian people, 90; religion contrasted with, 91; resistance in, 103–4

rationalization: of beauty standards, 83; double conscientiousness developed by, 4; Du Bois on, 48; patriarchal norms and, 45, 80; of SAMA women, 49; Selod on, 4
Ray, Krishnendu, 22
Rehman, Shehzeen: as influencer, 94; on social media, 92–93
religion: consumption framed by, 21, 72; culinary consumption influenced by, 29, 34–35, 79; fashion impacted by, 43, 57; homophobia and, 85; immigrants indicating, 36; Instagram revealing, 102; modesty norms in, 41, 53, 76; political opinion contrasted by, 91; social media and, 82, 92; travel indicating, 94; triple consciousness and, 49; wardrobe indicating, 93; wardrobe influenced by, 47–48, 54
religious identity, 61
resistance: in political opinion, 103–4; to socialization, 74

Al-Sadek, Maria Alia: Abdullah compared with, 91; on Instagram, 88–89; on modesty norms, 88

salwar kameez: identity indicated by, 93–94; SAMA women wearing, 53–54
SAMA women. *See* South Asian Muslim American women
second shift, 30–31
Sehimi, Sejal, 84–85
Shankar, Shalani, 7–8
Shirazi, F., 55
shopping: in Chicago, 13–14; community through, 99; on Facebook, 50; for fashion, 60, 64; for halal cooking, 31; on Hijabican, 77; identity formed through, 6; online, 6; SAMA women bonding through, 5–6, 46; on social media, 101–2; Zukin on, 5
socialization: of children, 33, 44; dietary restrictions in, 35; modesty norms in, 56–58; resistance to, 74; of SAMA

women, 52; social media in, 65; to status, 47

social media: African Americans on, 71; community created by, 70–71; consumption on, 15; discrimination on, 94; food on, 69; gender and, 65, 76; identity defined in, 67; influencer on, 15–16; Islam interpreted by, 74; modesty norms on, 73, 74, 95; Rehman on, 92–93; religion and, 82, 92; SAMA women on, 82, 86; shopping on, 101–2; in socialization, 65; social norms reinforced by, 72; triple consciousness on, 70

social norms, 72

South Asian Muslim American women (SAMA): African American compared to, 9; Arab Muslim contrasted with, 62; authenticity proved by, 9, 14, 25, 27; Brown Girl representing, 82–83; children impacting, 32–33; consumption by, 2, 12, 13–14; culinary consumption by, 17, 30, 32, 38; dietary restrictions of, 34–35, 39; discrimination impacting, 72, 87, 103, 104; fashion for, 16n1; fashion of, 41, 45–46; halal cooking by, 2, 21; wearing hijab, 43; hijab worn by, 54, 55–56; at H&M, 59; Indian people as, 13, 24; as influencers, 67; on Instagram, 75, 95; invisible labor of, 32; Latinos contrasted with, 11; luxury items bought by, 58; in Michigan, 65n1; in model minority, 11; modesty norms of, 57, 76; as mothers, 37; 9/11 impacting, 4; Pakistani people as, 13; patriarchal norms impacting, 33–34; rationalization of, 49; salwar kameez worn by, 53–54; second-generation, 13; second shift worked by, 30–31; Shankar on, 7–8; shopping bonding, 5–6, 46; socialization of, 52; social media, 82; on social media, 86; status of, 51; triple consciousness of, 2; during Trump administration, 15; Trump impacting, 97–98; women as, 1

Srinivas, Tulasi, 10, 25

status: Bourdieu on, 46; conspicuous consumption indicating, 97; consumption shaping, 65; fashion indicated by, 44–45; hijab influencing, 55; influencer using, 87; on Instagram, 68–69; luxury items indicating, 88; organic foods signaling, 40; of SAMA women, 51; socialization to, 47; wardrobe indicating, 43, 45–46, 100

Stewart, Martha, 23

thinness: in beauty standards, 77–78; in Bollywood, 83, 85; with colorism, 84; discrimination and, 81

third space identities: modesty norms in, 81; Muslim Girl and, 80–82; wardrobe in, 100

tradition: fashion preserving, 100; through food, 99

transnational feminism, 3

travel, 94

triple consciousness: on hijab, 62; after 9/11, 12; religion and, 49; of SAMA women, 2; on social media, 70; wardrobe influenced by, 48, 49–50

Trump, Donald, 97–98

Trump administration: discrimination under, 97–98; hijab influenced by, 90; identity impacted by, 62, 71; SAMA women during, 15

Veblen, Thorstein, 4–5
Vernon, Leah, 79

wardrobe: gender represented by, 52; of Harris, 105; identity and, 44, 51; modesty norms influencing, 58; nostalgia influencing, 61; religion indicated by, 93; religion influencing, 47–48, 54; status indicated by,

43, 45–46, 100; in third space identities, 100; triple consciousness influencing, 48, 49–50
West, Candace, 52
white people, 20, 23

Williams-Forson, Psyche, 3

zabiha, 36
Zimmerman, Don, 52
Zukin, Sharon, 5

About the Author

Farha Bano Ternikar is an associate professor of sociology and gender and women's studies at Le Moyne College, where she teaches gender and society, food and culture, and social inequality. She has published on the Indian immigrant family, halal food, and modesty norms. Born in London and raised in the United States, she is the daughter of Indian Muslim immigrants, and her research interests have been shaped by her family, the Muslim immigrant community in Florida, and the current political climate.

www.ingramcontent.com/pod-product-compliance
Lightning Source LLC
Chambersburg PA
CBHW020127010526
44115CB00008B/1017